Anonymous

Candid Thoughts

Or, an enquiry into the causes of national discontents and misfortunes

since the commencement of the present reign

Anonymous

Candid Thoughts
Or, an enquiry into the causes of national discontents and misfortunes since the commencement of the present reign

ISBN/EAN: 9783744793957

Printed in Europe, USA, Canada, Australia, Japan

Cover: Foto ©ninafisch / pixelio.de

More available books at **www.hansebooks.com**

CANDID THOUGHTS;

OR, AN

ENQUIRY INTO THE CAUSES

OF

NATIONAL DISCONTENTS

AND

MISFORTUNES

SINCE THE

COMMENCEMENT OF THE PRESENT REIGN.

———

LONDON:

Printed for W. NICOLL, No. 51, St. Paul's Church-yard,
1781.

CANDID THOUGHTS, &c.

IT is the duty of every good citizen to be well informed concerning the state of the nation. If grievances are complained of, or misfortunes announced, he will enquire with solicitude, whether they really exist or not, from what sources they proceed, and what remedies ought to be applied in order to redress and remove them.

Without comparing the state of this nation with what it has been in any former period, it cannot be denied, that, during the present reign, signal calamities have been mingled with our prosperity. The clamours of faction have been loud and inceffant. Jealousies and discontents have broken out in every part of the empire : a civil war, the most deplorable of all national disasters, has, for many years past, drained the blood and treasure of Britain ; a combination of the most powerful foreign enemies has aggravated and protracted these evils, and brought us to the brink of destruction.

To what causes are these to be ascribed ? Or who are the persons who have been instrumental in bringing them on ? The question will meet with different and contradictory solutions, according to the penetration, prejudices, and interest of those to whom it is referred. Men of narrow understanding are incapable of comprehending that complication of causes with which political events are

necessarily

neceffarily connected. Remote from the channels of information, thofe of fuperior judgment often indolently acquiefce in vague conjectures, and plaufible reprefentations, which are widely diftant from truth. Retainers to party, not only moft readily believe, but too often invent and induftrioufly fpread, fuch accounts of public meafures and the characters of men, as are the beft calculated to infure them fuccefs in their purfuits after that pre-eminence and power which they envy others the poffeffion of, and which they long to poffefs themfelves; or to fecure the enjoyment of thofe favorite objects, when fuccefs has once crowned their expectation.

To men of real integrity and patriotifm, (who it is ftill to be hoped make no inconfiderable proportion of the nation) to men who wifh to fix their judgment with candour, and to contribute to the true glory and welfare of their country, an attempt to inveftigate the caufes of thofe grievances and misfortunes, which have happened to the nation fince the commencement of this reign, may prove acceptable and ufeful. Such an attempt, purfued with impartiality and according to facts, though executed with flender ability, may, in fome meafure, affift them to diftinguifh between real and imaginary grievances, between fuch meafures as have been blamable or praife-worthy, either in the friends or enemies of adminiftration, to allay groundlefs fears and jealoufies, and to point out that conduct and thofe exertions, which the true intereft of their country demands. I enter on this undertaking with diffidence of my own abilities, but confiding in the rectitude of my intention, and the confcioufnefs of impartiality.

Our

Our prefent Sovereign afcended the throne at a moft aufpicious æra. There is not in the annals of Britain, an example of any reign having commenced with a concurrence of fo many circumftances, calculated to infure national profperity and the reciprocal affection and confidence of the Prince and his fubjects. Succefs, without interruption, had attended the Britifh arms for the two preceding years of the war. Our enemies, exhaufted and defponding, feemed to be compelled to reftore the peace of Europe upon whatever terms Britain fhould pleafe to dictate. A Prince born a Briton, claimed not only the allegiance, but the affections of his fubjects, and the commencement of his reign was marked with the unfeigned joy and heart-felt gratulations of a flourifhing and affectionate people.

It is painful at this hour to reflect, that many months of the new reign had not elapfed, till the murmurs of faction and difcord began to difturb that tranquillity, which the national fuccefs and the character of the Prince had encouraged us to expect. The caufes of this difappointment to the expectations of every good citizen, deferve to be inveftigated, and may be juftly confidered as the fources of many fucceeding misfortunes.

Firft, The attachment of the Sovereign to the Earl of Bute, was foon difplayed by fignal marks of confidence and favour. He was called from retirement to offices of public truft, and in a few months appeared in the moft important minifterial character. That the integrity and abilities of the man were intimately known to his mafter—that private friendfhip might be admitted to have fome influence in the choice—that it was candid to fufpend judgment, and to found approbation and

censure

cenfure upon the actual meafures purfued by the new minifter, were arguments which could not find entrance into the ears of thofe, who were ftung with the apprehenfion of lofing that influence and pre-eminence which they had fo long maintained. The power and preferment of Lord Bute, foon became an open and avowed topic of difcontent—his abilities were condemned before they were put to the proof—his country and his countrymen attacked with the moft virulent and licentious abufe. The indifcretion and the infolence of the favorites of Princes in former ages, and in circumftances widely different, were recited to roufe the terrors of the people. The impreffion of thefe arts of faction proved but too fuccefsful. Refignation fucceeded refignation. The council of the nation was divided more than it had been fince the beginning of the war, and at a time when the greateft vigour and moft cordial unanimity were required —the tranquillity of the Prince was difturbed—the minds of the people were poifoned. At the fame time, it is but candid to remark, that from the temper of the Englifh nation, from former examples in hiftory, and the influence of difappointed leaders of parties, all thefe difturbances might have been forefeen and expected, upon the fudden elevation and unrivalled influence of Lord Bute; and that nothing but neceffity, if fuch exifted, could have juftified him for advancing fo faft in the career of honours. I fay, nothing but neceffity could have juftified him, for it was often afferted, that the miniftry who had hitherto conducted the war with the greateft fpirit and fuccefs, difcovered but too great an inclination to protract it, however much the intereft of the nation called for peace. If this was the cafe, there might be

more

more patriotifm and difinterestednefs, and lefs imprudence and ambition in the conduct of Lord
Bute, than what his enemies have been willing to
admit. Certain however it is, that the promotion
of Lord Bute, from whatever motive it fprang,
whetted the edge of party fpirit, and gave birth
to animofities and jealoufies which have not yet
expired.

2. The odium of one minifter, the overgrown
popularity of another, introduced the prefent reign
with circumftances, which were by no means favorable to the duration of public tranquillity. The
abilities and fuccefs of Mr. Pitt can hardly be defcribed in terms of exaggeration. By the boldnefs
of his fpirit, and the vigor of enterprifes, a nation
lethargic, unfortunate, defponding, was quickly
exalted to a pitch of fplendor and glory unequalled
in the page of hiftory. If ever a minifter poffeffed
equal abilities, no one ever exerted them with
fuch aftonifhing fuccefs. He deferved the confidence and applaufe of the nation. The confidence
and applaufe of the nation were conferred upon
him without referve or limitation. Popularity and
fuccefs reciprocally promote each other. The demands of Mr. Pitt for fupplies, large beyond example, were gratified without a murmur, and the
effectual application of thefe, ftill heightned the
generofity of the people, and put into the hands
of the minifter fuch ample means of fuccefs as
fully outweighed fuperiority of numbers, and every
natural advantage upon the fide of our enemies.
At the commencement of this reign, the profperity of the nation, and the popularity of the man
who had been under Providence the inftrument of
that profperity, have attained to their meridian.

It

It is perhaps vain to expect in human characters, that degree of moderation, which is necessary to maintain virtue unshaken amidst an overflowing tide of applause and prosperity. It were easy to bring examples from history to shew, that great power and success have sometimes overturned those very virtues upon which they were originally erected. The law of Ostracism among the Athenians, though productive of injustice and ingratitude to individuals, was expedient in a political view, in order to curb exorbitant ambition, the offspring of success and popularity, and to preserve that balance of domestic influence which is the basis of free governments. But whatever apologies may be drawn from the infirmity of human nature, it cannot be denied, that the arrogance of Mr. Pitt became intolerable. He claimed a monopoly of influence and direction, disrespectful to the Sovereign, and disgusting to his partners in administration. His resignation ensued. He entered again the lifts of opposition. He had now acquired supreme authority over the minds of the people. His disapprobation alone was sufficient to stamp condemnation upon any public measure, and to render the authors of it suspected and odious. The use he made of this influence is but too well remembred. Did he ever, in one instance, approve of any plan of administration whilst he was out of place ? Did he ever cease to blast, with the thunder of his eloquence, the characters of those in power, and to thwart and confound every measure which he was not allowed to guide ? Hence the late peace, though concluded upon terms at least as favorable as those which he himself had dictated, was assumed as full evidence of the ignorance and wickedness of the administration

who

who succeeded him. Hence the repeal of the stamp act in America, and all the mighty mischiefs it has since brought forth. Whether this repeal was expedient or not, is a question which may occur in a subsequent part of these considerations. The fact I believe is well known. The repeal of the stamp act was, in a great measure, owing to the influence of Mr. Pitt. A new administration, in the most important question that ever affected the interests of this nation, were determined to embrace his opinion, in order to insure that stability which they could not expect from their own wisdom and merits. But to return particularly to the conduct of Mr. Pitt. If he would not agree to continue in administration, upon any terms consistent with the honour of the Prince and the respect due to his colleagues : if it was his determined plan, when he was himself out of power, to oppose those who were in power, it might have been naturally expected, and has been felt in experience, that neither caution, nor virtue, nor intentions however upright, could render any ministry, or any set of men, invulnerable by his attacks. Hence he had the fatal success to keep alive a distrust and jealousy of every future administration—he traversed and perplexed every measure going forward—he robbed his country of that established peace and pleasing confidence, which the government of the mildest of Princes ought to have produced—he divided the children from the father. If Chatham had not approved, a feeble opposition would not have dared even to have whispered an apology for the rebellion of America. Had he with his tropes and figures fenced the supremacy of the British Parliament, that man must have hazarded his blood who would

have

have prefumed to contravert the doctrine, and
bring it to the teft of argument. A rabble without arms, or difcipline, or money, might, fecure
from danger, take the field againft the veterans
who had conquered for them a few years before,
and might bid defiance to the threats, the power,
and the wealth of Britain, whilft the man, who
with defpotic fway reigned over the opinions of
the people, abetted their caufe and applauded their
virtue.

How myfterious are the ways of Providence! That
the fame man fhould build up and pull down—
that the glory and fhame of a nation fhould ftand
fo near to one another, be exhibited upon the fame
theatre, and affected by the fame inftrument—
furely there is in this fomewhat rare and unac-
countable! How ignorantly do we often wifh for
the continuance of life? If that of Mr. Pitt had
ended with his adminiftration, would his abilities
or integrity have been leffened in the eftimation
either of his friends or his enemies? It is impoffible to confine our judgment to any detached part
of a man's life and character. We look backward
and forward, and from actions previous and fucceeding, our praife or cenfure of feparate parts is
raifed or diminifhed.

They who are fond of moralizing, and of drawing ufeful inftructions from the various events
which occur in the hiftory of nations, might perhaps in the oppofite effects of Lord Chatham's
conduct, read the vengeance of heaven againft an
impious and corrupt people—that the idol fhould
fall and crufh thofe who bowed before it—that a
nation who put her whole confidence in the arm of
one man, and neither looked up to Providence in
truft or gratitude for fuccefs—that the fame nation
fhould

should be depreſſed by the very arm that had exalted her—that by his councils ſhe ſhould be perſuaded to renounce all the fruits of glory which his abilities had acquired—that from him ſhe ſhould learn the language, of deſpondency, and tamely ſubmit to diſgrace and mortification. That all this ſhould happen to Great-Britain, appears a diſpenſation of Providence ſo rare and ſignal, and in its nature and effects ſo ſuitable and adequate, to the ſpecies of our crime, that we may admit the moſt ſerious application of it, without falling under the reproach of a ſuperſtitious and gloomy imagination.

3. The admiſſion of Tories into a ſhare of adminiſtration, has often been urged as a ground of diſcontent under the preſent reign, and has had its effect in exciting jealouſies in the breaſts of many of his Majeſty's well affected ſubjects. From the acceſſion of the Houſe of Hanover, with a very few exceptions, the Whigs only have been admitted to offices of public truſt.

Though the Tories concurred in the revolution, took the oaths to King William, and were afterwards chiefly inſtrumental in bringing about the act of ſettlement, * yet it has been taken for granted, that the Whigs were more ſincerely attached to the Hanoverian family, and the conſtitution of government formed at the revolution. It has likewiſe been alledged, that moſt of the avowed and ſuſpected friends of the Pretender, were to be found amongſt the Tories, who were alſo

* The ſucceſſion of the Houſe of Hanover to the crown of Britain, was enacted by Parliament 1701, when a Tory miniſtry was in power, and Mr. Harley, Speaker of the Houſe of Commons, took the principal lead in that buſineſs See Bur-net.

alſo ſuppoſed to have maintained principles oppoſite to the eſtabliſhed ſyſtem of laws and government. Hence as a predelicttion for Whig miniſters,
was extremely natural to Sovereigns of the Hanoverian family, ſo an excluſion of the oppoſite faction ſeemed juſtifiable in a political view and upon
conſtitutional principles. The admiſſion of Tories
into adminiſtration was therefore an innovation,
and a ſpecious topic of objecttion held forth to the
jealous and diſcontented. To employ them was
repreſented as a meaſure of ingratitude, and a pre-
lude to arbitrary power.

In a nation where the liberty of the preſs is in-
dulged almoſt without reſtricttion, there is not a
meaſure of government that may not be repreſented in ſuch a light, as to raiſe the alarm and
diſcontent of the people. The great body of
mankind are incapable of tracing effects through
the labyrinth of political cauſes—they are influenced by paſſion more than by reaſon—it is only
neceſſary to aſcribe to any meaſure conſequences
which they abhor, in order to inliſt them in a determined oppoſition to the meaſure itſelf. This is
more eſpecially the caſe where the predominant
paſſion interferes. Men, who in other inſtances
give full proof of underſtanding and penetration,
will often appear deaf to the voice of reaſon when
under the influence of the over-ruling paſſion.
Nations as well as individuals are ſubject to ſuch
an influence. In France, affecttion to the perſon
of the monarch—in Britain, attachment to liberty
and the conſtitution (a more ſubſtantial object)
bears irreſiſtible ſway over the inclinations of the
people. To render any meaſure therefore deteſt-
able to the people of England, it need only be
repreſented as dangerous to liberty. The admiſſion
of

of Tories to adminiſtration was repreſented as dangerous to liberty. Was it ſo in reality? Let us not be carried away with the violent clamour of faction—let us hear the calm voice of reaſon.

To exclude any denomination or body of men from ſharing in the truſt and honour of adminiſtration, farther than as they are defective in the principles or abilities eſſential to the faithful diſcharge of them,. is equally repugnant to juſtice and ſound policy—to entail infamy and the frowns of the Sovereign upon particular families, and to puniſh the children for the iniquities of the fathers, if they have not been partakers of the guilt of their fathers, is a rule of government againſt which every upright heart muſt revolt. In vain do we boaſt of the excellence of our conſtitution, if it is calculated for the narrow purpoſe of raiſing one part of the community upon the ruins of another. Where is juſtice if you find guilt without a proof, or impute to men thoſe very principles which they profeſs to abjure and deteſt. The moment when any party of men are known to depart from the dangerous prejudices of their fathers, that moment the partition wall ſhould be broken down, and they ought to be promiſcuouſly taken in, to partake with their fellow citizens in the common honours and emoluments of the ſtate.

An excluſive plan of governing is no leſs inconſiſtent with ſound policy. If the Tories were ſuſpected of diſaffection either to the Prince or conſtitution, it might have been a queſtion whether a well guarded confidence, and moderate ſhare of truſt, might not have proved the moſt ſucceſsful method to conquer their prejudices and conciliate their affections. Diſgrace and mortifications affixed to any denomination of men, by cuſtom cuftom and the profeffed maxims of thofe in power, only rankle in their breafts, and render them vigilant to feize the firft opportunity to overturn that government, under which they find themfelves ftigmatized and oppreffed. The Roman method of profcription, though more cruel, was more political; as it effected the total extirpation of thofe, who were known to have any intereft or wifhes incompatable with the power and fafety of the perfons who had got into their hands the reins of government. That the happy day for abolifhing all diftinctions, for reconciling juftice with good policy, and uniting all claffes of men in affection to the family upon the throne, was arrived at the commencement of this reign, will, I think, be obvious to every one who candidly attends to the following obfervations: The fpirit of liberty has been fpreading and gathering ftrength in this nation, fince the happy æra of the revolution. Enlargement of fentiment with refpect to political fubjects, unknown in former times, is now difcovered among all ranks of men. The common rights of mankind are better underftood. Queftions relating to the intereft of the people, formerly intricate and doubtful, or wilfully embarraffed and kept in fufpence by minifters, are now cleared up and defined with precifion. A blind attachment to prerogative, is hardly to be found among any clafs of men; and the laws are univerfally admitted as the only rule of royal authority. All men are more or lefs tinctured with the prevailing fentiments of the times. Tories, or thofe who are called fuch, but who ought more properly to be called the children of Tories, are now profeffed friends to liberty and the conftitution.

If

If any man still obstinately contends for a distinction of families—I ask him how it is possible to ascertain that distinction? Have Whigs and Tories, like the different Indian coasts, inclosed themselves within certain barriers never to be broken down, and prohibited intermarriages with those who are not of their own class and way of thinking? Whilst the name of a political distinction has been retained, has not the blood of those to whom it is affixed, intermingled in their posterity? If guilt runs down in the blood of Tories, let the pedigree of families be traced, and how few of those who boast of the name of Whigs will be found untainted with the contagion. Nothing but the absurdity can equal the injustice and illiberality of perpetuating the distinction between Whig and Tory.

If after all it should be insisted upon, that a manifest preference is given to Tories, which has turned the balance of power to their side, I would desire any man who is of this opinion, carefully to inspect the Court Register of every year since the accession of his Majesty to the throne—after the best information he can obtain about the pedigree of persons who fill the lists of offices, he will perhaps find it not a little perplexing to decide under what standard they fall to be marshalled—but should he, after the most deliberate calculation, resolve, that the names of Tories out-number those of the Whigs, and that the scale of power inclines to their side, yet in justice it still becomes him to enquire, whether this ought not to be imputed to accidental causes, and the caprice of faction, more than to the influence of a minister, or the inclination or fixed purpose of the Prince? When the distinction between Whig and Tory was invidiously revived

revived at the beginning of the present reign, it was the avowed resolution of some of the most eminent Whig families, not to take any part in administration unless the Tories were utterly cast out. The necessary effect of this resolution, under the government of a Prince determined not to sacrifice equity to faction, must have been to diminish the number of Whigs, and to increase that of Tories, who enjoyed places of administration. But in such a case does not the Prince stand acquitted of all charge of partiality, and ought not the decline of the interest of the Whigs to be fairly imputed to their own obstinacy, pique, and resentment?

4. The troubles which have befallen the nation in the present reign, are, without any controversy, to be imputed, in a great proportion, to relaxation in the executive power, which has tamely looked on, whilst licentiousness, in every corner of the empire, has swoln to a pitch incompatible with the order, peace and dignity of government. What was there that the most malicious ingenuity could invent, in order to losen the affections of the people from the Prince, to vilify the persons of ministers, and render government contemptible and odious, that was not actually said and written, and published at the beginning of this reign. We know that no private character can bid defiance to the attacks of malice. There is in human nature a propensity to believe the worst, and even the most candid are but too ready to think that bold assertions, to the disadvantage of a man's character, are not altogether without foundation. Misrepresentations of the conduct of persons in stations of public trust, are still more successfully injurious, through the additional influence of envy, and that

jealousy

jealoufy of liberty, which is the characteriftic of British fubjects. Can it be doubted that the minds of the people have been perverted, and their confidence in government fhaken, by that outrage of abufe which has broken down all the fences of dignity and innocence, with which the moft refpectable characters in this nation are furrounded? The fuccefs of Mr. Wilkes, and the afcendant he acquired in the metropolis of this kingdom, are notorious proofs, that there are feafons when neither falfhood nor profligacy in any degree counteract the virulence of the poifon which they diffufe. Ought not fome meafures to have been adopted, in order to ftop fuch enormous licentioufnefs? Is not a certain veneration due to the magifterial character? Is not a certain degree of confidence in rulers neceffary, to give fuccefs to thofe plans which they are carrying forward with a view to the public good? Can it ferve the caufe of the nation, in any inftance, to confound all diftinction between right and wrong—to call faction liberty, law tyranny, and to afcribe the very worft motives to the beft intentions? Shall the reputation of every private man be guarded by law, and fhall the meaneft and moft abandoned of the people be fuffered, with impunity, to affaffinate the character of the Prince?

If the evils complained of are already provided againft by law, why was not the law put in execution? If, in this refpect, the laws already exifting are weak and defective, juftice and found policy require that they fhould be reformed and invigorated. That the ftatutes already enacted were fufficient to curb fuch outrage of licentioufnefs, may be inferred from facts upon record. Any one who will be at pains to confult the State Trials,

B

since the accession of the Hanoverian family, will
find, that the severest censures of law have been
inflicted upon the authors and publishers of writings, which are reserved and cautious, in compa-
rison with those which have daily circulated under
the present reign, without the notice or controul
of persons in power. * Here then the persons in-
vested with the executive power must certainly
have been in fault, and to their neglect and timidity we must, in some measure, impute the enormous progress of licentiousness and slander, and
the discontents, jealousies and hatreds, which these
have disseminated in the hearts of the people.

Am I then an enemy to the liberty of the press?
God forbid! I am only an enemy to calumny, to
injustice and disorder. Let every man be permitted not only to think for himself, but let him do
all he can to persuade others to think as he does.
Let the conduct of ministers be examined with a
jealous scrutiny—let their errors be published
through the whole nation—let the bell of alarm be
sounded the moment that one peg of the glorious
fabric of our constitution is touched—but let public as well as private virtue be protected from the
wounds of calumny—let honour be given to whom
honour is due. Is the crime of malice and false-
hood extenuated by the dignity of the person against
whom it is levelled, or the extent of the mischief
which it means to produce? Shall the assassin, in
order to mitigate the severity of law, plead that
he hurt not the extremities, but thrust a dagger
into the very heart and seat of life. Away with
that

---

* The fate of Atterbury, Sacheverel, Mathews the printer,
and Shebbeare, warrants this assertion.—Compare the most exceptionable passages in their writings with the North-Briton,
Letters of Junius, &c. &c.

that liberty of the prefs, which defeats the very end
which it was intended to ferve. The liberty of the
prefs was intended to inform the people, to remove
that ignorance which is the mother of flavery, as
well as of fuperftition. This privilege is certainly
abufed when the people are mifinformed, and inftead of being animated to contend for their rights,
are inflamed by a tumultuous rage, which threatens the deftruction of that conftitution upon which
their liberty and privileges depend. The lofs of
fight is a deplorable calamity, but to all purpofes
of ufe and fafety in life, a man had better be blind,
than have eyes which mifreprefent external objects,
and level the precipice towards which he is moving
without apprehenfion of danger.

But the intolerable licentioufnefs of the prefs is
not the only evidence of that feeblenefs and relaxation of government, which has marked the conduct of fucceeding adminiftrations in the prefent
reign. We have feen in the compafs of a few
years many enquiries carried on, with refpect to
mifmanagement of truft, abufe of power, mifconduct of Generals and Admirals—but has ever one
of thefe been brought to an effectual iffue—nay,
have they not ferved as frefh evidences of the im-
potency and fatality of government, and encouraged future delinquents, without the dread of
punifhment, to run out into more extravagant acts
of irregularity and abufe, in the departments with
which they have been intrufted? The riots in
Bofton upon enacting the ftamp duty, afterwards
at New-York upon quartering the foldiers in bar-
racks, and again at Bofton upon exacting the duty
on tea, were all fuffered to pafs with impunity.
What had government to expect but the repetition
and increafe of infults? A narrow compafs of experience

perience is fufficient to evince, ...at imprudent and
unfeafonable lenity is productive of the moft extenfive mifchief and cruelty to the very perfons
towards whom it is exercifed. Is it not confirmed
by the hiftory of all popular affemblies, that after
they have been in the habit of violating the eftablifhed laws, and have loft all refpect for magiftrates, conceffions only ferve to multiply demands,
to aggravate their infolence and rage, and finally
to fubvert all lawful authority? A flight exertion
of the executive arm, perhaps a fingle example of
chaftifement directed by the ftrict rules of equity
and law, might have mercifully prevented that
deluge of blood which has already been fhed in
the conteft between Britain and her Colonies. Had
members of parliament in oppofition levelled their
attacks againft the weak fide of adminiftration—
had they cenfured delays, fluctuation of councils,
conceffions derogatory to the honour of the nation
and Prince—the wifhes of the moft virtuous and
difinterefted of the people might have infured their
fuccefs, and they might have proved the happy
inftruments of averting or alleviating the heavy
calamities under which we groan. But, alas! unhappy nation! from this very quarter has been
derived the increafe and confirmation of public
diftrefs—which leads me to obferve,

5. That the immorality or want of principle in
oppofition, has been the moft fertile fource of
national adverfity. It is an old obfervation, that
the higheft outrage of iniquity can only be attained
by mankind in a focial and confederated ftate.
The affociation of numbers allays the fears, and
animates the courage of the individual. Difgrace
and danger feem to be leffened or totally annihilated, by being fcattered and divided among the
multitude,

multitude, and in compenſation for the loſs of that
legitimate applauſe, which is only due to virtue,
they have erected among themſelves a bank of
ſpurious fame, which is paid out in proportion to
the boldneſs and ſucceſs with which each member
purſues the intereſt of the party to which he clings.
Thus men who are leagued in political faction,
run headlong into thoſe meaſures, which, if left to
themſelves, they could neither have contrived, nor
dared to own. It will be difficult to find in the
hiſtory of this or any other kingdom, an example
of faction more diſhonourable, inconſiſtent and
outrageous, than that which has embarraſſed the
meaſures of adminiſtration in the moſt critical
juncture of affairs. I ſhall juſt mention a few of
thoſe characteriſtics which mark the groſs immorality of oppoſition in parliament, from the beginning of the preſent reign, and particularly of late
years, during our unhappy conteſt with our Colonies.

Oppoſition, from the beginning of this reign,
has been a thing too much perſonal. Inſtead of
oppoſing the men upon account of the meaſures,
the meaſures, whatever they be, are oppoſed and
contradicted upon account of the men who propoſe them. In the late reign (upon which I mean
to throw no reflections) the oppoſition to Sir Robert Walpole's adminiſtration was founded upon
principle, and had for its object the overthrow of
an avowed and notorious ſyſtem of corruption.
But ſuch is now the contention and eagerneſs of
oppoſition, that they have not only waſted time
and forfeited dignity, by deſcending to the moſt
frivolous topics of debate, but have croſſed meaſures of evident utility to the nation, and have
even ſometimes been reduced to the awkward ſitu-

ation

ation of traducing thofe very plans which they themfelves contrived. *

In all former inftances of oppofition, it was a determined plan to watch with a critical eye the conduct of thofe perfons, to whom adminiftration had entrufted the executive part of government—hence the moft powerful motive to render minifters cautious and difinterefted in the choice of their fervants, and hence the greateft inducement to thefe to perform their duty with diligence, fidelity and vigour. It was almoft impoffible that any example of remiffnefs or mifconduct or treachery, could efcape with impunity. And hence by this plan, from whatever principle it proceeded, the public fuccefs and welfare were promoted. Directly the reverfe of this have been the plan and effects of the late oppofition in parliament. To diftrefs adminiftration, they have not fcrupled to facrifice the intereft of the nation, and have uniformly taken into their protection every man who has been unfuccefsful or treacherous in the difcharge of duty.

Oppofition has laboured to deprefs the fpirits of the nation, by expofing and magnifying all her weakneffes and danger. The child, whofe heart is infpired with a fenfe of filial veneration and gratitude, will be flow and reluctant to apprehend the danger which threatens that life which is to him moft precious and defirable. Which is to be accounted the true patriot, the man who beholds
with

---

* Recollect the enquiry concerning Greenwich hofpital—Oppofition to the bill for taking away the privilege of the fervants of members of parliament—The high tone of dignity they affumed about the affair of Falkland Ifland—The abafing terms in which they have fpoken of the ftrength and refources of Britain fince the commencement of the American war.

with sorrow the wounds of his country, and touches them with a gentle hand, and pours in balm to soften and to heal them—or he who lays them open to the derision and insult of those who have inflicted them, and by the rudeness with which he handles them, and the neglect of timely and proper remedies, gives them a deadly effect.

The immorality of opposition has been most glaring, from the methods to which they have resorted, in order to shake the fabric of administration. Unable to make any impression by argument and fair attack, they have employed unlawful and violent weapons—they have called associations, and encouraged tumults, and put the minds of the people into a state of fermentation, at a period of emergency, which required the undisturbed and cordial co-operation of all classes of men.

The immorality of opposition, appears from the grossest inconsistency in the conduct of individuals who stand foremost in the list of its champions. It is impossible to conceive a more perfect contradiction of sentiments and language, than what has been declared by the leaders of minority in both houses of parliament. We have beheld the very men, who founded the subjection of America to the British parliament without limitation, and who confirmed that subjection by a declaratory statute, in the course of a few years approving of a rebellion in America, upon account of a slight exaction of supply in conformity to that statute. *

We

* The Marquis of Rockingham was first lord of the treasury, and General Conway secretary of state, when an act passed, intitled, " An act for the better securing the dependence of his " Majesty's dominions in America upon the crown of Britain."

This

We have feen the man who propofed the American tax, or who prefided in adminiftration when it was propofed, and who ftill purfued confiftent conduct, after he had retired from office, by defending the meafure, and contending for the neceffity, of enforcing the fubmiffion of America by power of arms—we have feen that very man, who thus defended the juftice and neceffity of the American war, at laft condemning another adminiftration for fuftaining the caufe which he had begun, and, like a cowardly and treacherous general, turning

This act declares, That the King and Parliament of Britain had, hath, and of right ought to have, full power and authority to make laws and flatutes of fufficient force to bind the Colonies and his Majefty's fubjects in them, in all cafes whatfoever.

General Conway declared in the Houfe of Commons, October the 26th, in the debate upon American affairs, That he wifhed to fee the declaratory act repealed—Why?—Was it becaufe he thought it wrong, and was in his heart againft it?—By no means, for he added, It had been paffed under his aufpices, and on abftract, legal principles, he thought it right, and at the time of paffing it proper and neceffary.

If this diftinction between what is really right, and what is fo on abftract, legal principles, is admitted, it were to be wifhed that the legiflature, as often as it declares any of the rights of the crown or parliament, would at the fame time give fome hint, by which it might be conjectured to which of thefe they refer, and whether they have decided upon abftract and legal, or upon plain and practical principles, left the executive fervants of government fhould miftake, and fpeculate, where it was meant that they fhould act—or rafhly act, where it was meant that they fhould only fpeculate. If this diftinction is once admitted, the fcience of law muft become tenfold more vague and intricate. The ftudent muft not reft fatisfied with collecting and remembering facts, which, from their number and variety, afforded fufficient labour to the mind—but he muft pry into the hearts of legiflators, he muft detect mental refervation, he muft diftinguifh between what is right and proper in an abftract and practical view. Some compenfation of amufement, however, he will derive from the fcope that is given to ingenuity and imagination, employed in the place of judgment.

turning his back and deserting his soldiers in the very heat and extremity of the attack to which he had led them on. * We have seen the very man, who

* Duke of Grafton.—It was very extraordinary (said Mr. Burke in his celebrated speech upon American affairs, May 8, 1770) that the great person who was the foremost for repealing the stamp act, and that too upon the principles of the Americans themselves, should, when he found himself at the head of ministry, be the very person to invent a new system of taxes upon the Colonies ; and it is very certain, that at that period his Grace never disavowed the charge. Nay, after he resigned his office of first lord of the treasury, he made a public declaration, that he would continue to support the measures of government. The American measures, or measures relating to America, were the most important which were at that time agitated in parliament ; and it is but a fair construction to suppose, that he had these in his view—his subsequent conduct confirms this construction—for he was as good as his word, and for two years urged the necessity of coercive measures against America. It is true, his Grace afterwards declared, (October 25, 1775) that he had been deceived and misled to give his countenance to measures which he never approved, and in particular that of coercing America by force of arms—and he afterwards declared, that he had been secretly, or in his own mind, against the plan of taxing America, and had suggested the plan of drawing back one shilling per pound in Britain, and imposing threepence per pound in America upon tea, as a species of tax the least obnoxious. May not Lord North, Lord Hillsborough, Lord George Germaine, or any other person in ministry, make the same declaration some years hence, when they are displaced, or quarrel with their colleag·· in office? Was not this language from one who had been prime minister, and which was suffered to pass without reprehension, a very dangerous precedent, as it was in effect disclaiming responsibility? Suppose the total alienation of America from Britain, and that an enraged nation should call for an impeachment of the minister, or ministers, who were the authors of those measures which had occasioned the rending of the empire—it would be impossible for the most impartial to acquit any one who has presided at the helm of affairs since the commencement of this present reign, for all of them are guilty, nor would it be easy to determine to which of them the greatest share of guilt ought to be apportioned—whether to him who moved the stamp act, or

to

who formerly fpoke of the people in terms of contempt which no provocation could juftify, and
who devoted the whole power of his eloquence to
defend what was, perhaps, one of the moft violent
encroachments upon the liberties of the people,
that miniftry have dared to attempt fince the period of the revolution—we have feen that very
man, when degraded into the clafs of the people,
addreffing them in terms of the moft ftrained adu-
lation, prompting them to the moft exorbitant,
unconftitutional claims, and afcribing to them
rights which annihilated the very ufe of reprefentation. * When fuch fudden and entire change of
fentiments

to him who repealed it, and fubftituted the declaratory ftatute ;
ot to him who relinquifhed abftract views, and reduced that ftatute to practice, and impofed the tax upon tea ; or finally to him
who commenced war againft America, denying fubordination,
and refilling the power of Britain, and who continued that war
after the interefts of America were entwined with thofe of our
hereditary and moft inveterate enemies. In thefe views, according to the received doctrine of refponfibility, every minifter
ftands forth an object of guilt—but allow the fame privilege
which the Duke of Grafton has claimed, give them credit for
private fentiments and opinions, directly contrary to thofe meafures which were carried on under their adminiftration, and
which were never heard of till the worft effects of them were ex-
perienced, and without remedy—let them proteft againft re-
trofpective views, and draw the curtain of oblivion upon the
paft, and fall in with the current of popular fentiments, and
impeachment can have no object, guilt is done away, and an
injured nation difappointed of her refentment.

* Mr. Fox was the man who appeared upon the huftings at
Brentford, and put up Colonel Luttrell in oppofition to Mr.
Wilkes, May 1769. He afterwards took the principal lead in
the debate for the propriety and lawfulnefs of approving Colonel
Luttrell's election, though he had only 296 votes, and Mr. Wilkes
1043. He was the great champion for that meafure in all future
debates upon that fubject. When in adminiftration he was a
great oppofer of Mr. Sawbridge's motion for triennial parliaments.
He

sentiments attends the loss of power, who can hesitate to pronounce to what motive it ought in justice to be assigned? Who does not see, that in such men patriotism, like the religion of the hypocrite, is put on to serve a turn? Is not even the pretence of sincerity in such men, an insult to the understanding of every person of honour and penetration? Does not such glaring versatility and self-contradiction, to persons at a distance from the immediate scene of political exhibitions, suggest most melancholy reflections concerning the state of virtue in the most illustrious assembly of the nation? Must not virtue indeed be at a low ebb, where such impudent violation of integrity and honour is expressed without shame, and heard without indignation?

6. The American war from the beginning, and in its progress till this day, has been pregnant with the most dreadful calamities to the British empire. It is not to be expected, that any new matter can be offered upon a subject that has engaged the thoughts of every political writer for the last six years of this reign. At the same time, this Enquiry would be greatly defective, should it pass
in

He has since professed a recantation of his former principles. Mr. Fox said, I will never acknowledge the voice of the people to be fully expressed any where but in this House. [See his speech upon the commitment of the Lord Mayor, March 27, 1771.] What did he not say in the course of last session to enforce respect for associations of the people? No man, at the commencement of these disturbances, spoke in a more decisive tone of the right of the British parliament to tax America, or contended more vehemently for coercive measures, or treated of the power of the Americans, in more vilifying and contemptuous terms. The justice of their cause, and the magnitude of the power of these thirteen paltry provinces, have lately been drawn by him in the most glowing colours. Mr. Fox was burnt in effigy at Boston.

in silence an event which men of whatever parties and interests agree in admitting to be the principal cause of national distress. That we may not misplace censure or applause, or mistake the remedy which our circumstances require, it is necessary that I should offer somewhat upon this subject, avoiding at the same time tediousness of argument and intricacy of reasoning, and insisting concisely upon those facts and observations which are most obvious and uncontrovertible.

The state of security in which the American Colonies were placed by the late peace—their successful resistance to the stamp act—the illicit gain of smugglers, uncontroled by a more vigorous execution of law—the ambitious views of individuals, and the prevalence of faction at home, all concurred to render it probable, that a plan of introducing or extending taxes in America, would meet with the most obstinate and violent opposition. Was this plan just and equitable ? Was it wise and expedient ? If it was not just and equitable, no prospect of gain to Britain ought to have moved the proposal of it—it might be just and yet inexpedient, if it could not be compassed without expence of blood and treasure, which no success in the issue could repay. Let us give our attention to each of these questions—first, Was this plan just and equitable ?

That every state ought to contribute to the support of that government by which it is protected, is a maxim of justice so obvious, that no argument can render it more clear and convincing. That America ought to contribute to the revenue of Britain, in a proportion adequate to the real expences laid out by Britain for her defence and protection, is a particular application of a general, clear,

clear, and uncontroverted propofition. But be-
fides compenfation for the annual expence of protection to America, was not fomething more due
upon the ftrict footing of juftice? If America grew
up to wealth and profperity under the munificent
aid and protection of Britain, was not fome proportion of that wealth a due return for fuch aid and
protection? If this protection had been merely declaratory, inert and inexpenfive--if the name of
the alliance of Britain had been barely fufficient,
to have overawed the nations who had any intereft
or wifh, to difturb the peace of our Colonies advancing to ftrength and profperity—in fuch circumftances we muft have appealed to gratitude
rather than to juftice, and our claims muft have
been propofed with greater moderation and referve.
But if on the contrary, the welfare of America has
been a coftly caufe—if the blood and money of
Britain have been profufely wafted for her defence
and fecurity—if the late war was chiefly undertaken
in her behalf, and added an accumulation of mil-
lions to the debt of the nation—if Britain was
loaded with new and oppreffive taxes to difcharge
the intereft of that debt—was it unjuft or tyrannical to call for the affiftance of America, or demand
a tax in order to alleviate the weight of a burden
incurred upon her account? Was it in America
either generous or fair to refufe to comply with
this demand, and to vouchfafe that aid which juftice and the neceffity of the Mother Country required? Thefe are plain obfervations, and ftrike
every man of common underftanding.

I know only of two objections which may be
brought to invalidate the force of the arguments
which I have now adduced : firft, It has been afferted that Great-Britain, by her exclufive trade
with

with the Colonies, and the reſtrictions ſhe has impoſed upon their manufactures and exports, has
derived profits which have fully indemnified all
her care and expence in rearing and defending
them. But even this view of the ſubject being
admitted, it is evident, that a diſtinction ought to
be made between ſuch reſtrictions of commerce as
were equally advantageous to the Mother Country
and her Colonies, and thoſe which were only advantageous to Britain, and perhaps injurious to
the wealth and proſperity of America. Might not
commercial laws and reſtrictions be framed for the
double purpoſe of promoting at once the intereſt of
Britain and her dependent Colonies. If, for inſtance, it was the privilege and advantage of the
Britiſh trader to furniſh the Colonies with every
ſpecies of manufactured commodities, it was in
their infant ſtate no leſs the intereſt of the Colonies
to have full dependence upon Britain for the ſup-
ply of theſe. Clearing, cultivation of lands, and
population, could not have advanced with ſuch
amazing rapidity, if their attention had been divided, and called off to the various manufactures
neceſſary for cloathing, furniture, and the work of
plantation. If, on the other hand, any reſtrictions
of trade impoſed by the authority of parliament,
originally were, or from a change of circumſtances
had grown to be unequal or hurtful to the true intereſt of the Colonies, here was a real grievance,
and a juſt and proper ground of complaint and petition for redreſs. Let ſuch complaints be heard—
let ſuch reſtrictions be abrogated—let ſuch grievances be redreſſed. Away with the plan of drawing, from reſtrictions illiberal and oppreſſive, a
compenſation for claims that ſtand upon the firm
and broad foundations of juſtice and equity. Let
all

all the fubjects of the empire be placed upon the
fame level—let them enjoy the fame privileges—
let the Colonies be permitted to turn to the beft
account all that God and nature, and their own
induftry, have put into their hands. And in this
view the doctrine of the great Mr. Pitt, when the
argument of American taxation was moved in parliament, appeared illiberal and unfatisfactory.
" Reftrain (faid he) their trade as much as you
pleafe, not a horfe-nail fhall be made in America,
but not one farthing of tax." At beft, it was a
plan of difguifed injuftice. Had he inverted the
propofition—Enlarge their trade, encourage their
manufactures, demand taxes in a fair and equitable
proportion, (which would have amounted to the
fame effect) with a propofal to give them all the
privileges and all the burdens of Britifh fubjects,
I fhould have entertained a better opinion of the
foundnefs of his judgment, and the generofity of
his heart.

But fuppofe that profit, or money, or compenfation from America, (give it whatever appellation
you chufe) whether by tax or trade was equally
confonant to juftice, yet there are many obvious
and ftrong reafons for preferring the mode of exaction by tax, to that by reftriction upon trade.
The former is a more plain and direct way of raifing money, and may be contrived fo as to fall in-
difcriminately upon all ranks of men—it does not
expofe the veracity and morals of the fubjects to
fuch extreme temptation and danger—the quan-
tum may be afcertained with greater precifion, and
rendered effectual in one way or other. Reftric-
tions upon trade are more eafily evaded, and fub-
mitted to only fo long as they are not inconfiftent
with the interefts of the perfons upon whom they
are

are impofed. They fall heavy in the firft inftance upon the commercial body of men, who poffefs a great proportion of the wealth and power of the nation—they eftablifh open hoftility between them and the revenue officers, which is too eafily and frequently transferred to the conftituents. By feducing felfifh men into perjury, the moft confummate act of guilt, they render them an eafy prey to every inferior fpecies of iniquity, and at laft fubvert the morals of the people.

But it was not the tax, but the impofition of it by the authority of parliament, that was condemned by many of the friends of America on this fide of the Atlantic. The injuftice of taxation, without reprefentation, was the argument urged by Mr. Pitt for the repeal of the ftamp act. It is not to my purpofe, at prefent, to expofe the refinement of that diftinction, which was currently admitted, between legiflation and taxation; nor fhall I undertake, in this place, what I think it were no difficult tafk to demonftrate, that legiflation without reprefentatives, is at leaft as unreafonable and unjuft, as taxation without reprefentatives; and that there is not any mifchief or danger fufpected from any one of thefe branches of authority, that may not as reafonably be inferred from the other. A power of legiflation, uncontrouled by the negative voice of the people over whom it is exercifed, would furely prove as fit an inftrument of oppreffion as the moft arbitrary monarch ever wifhed to get into his hands. I obferve, in general, that if the fcheme of taxation was once admitted to be juft, reafonable, and neceffary, an exception to the particular mode or plan of carrying it into execution, could never juftify any individual or fet of men, in purfuing mea-

fures which evidently tended to fruftrate or overturn the plan itfelf. When the American tax
became the univerfal topic of converfation, about
a dozen years ago, I hardly ever mixed with any
company where a variety of opinions did not
occur, and where different plans were not fug-
gefted, in the freedom of fpeculation, and perhaps
after all, however oppofite to one another, there
was not one of them for which fomething plaufible in the way of argument might not be faid,
and againft which fomething plaufible in the way
of objection might not be thrown out. In fhort,
of fchemes and fpeculations there is no end. If
the juftice and neceffity of taxing America were
once admitted, what appeared the leaft exceptionable, or the moft conftitutional plan of carrying
it into effect? Has not the parliament, fince the
revolution, been underftood to be invefted with
fupreme legiflative authority over Britain, and all
her dominions? Would it then have been fafe in
any minifter to have departed from the fixed,
conftitutional mode of taxation?

I acknowledge, that members of the Britifh
parliament, as it is now conftituted, could not
be underftood to have the fame intimate connection with the provinces of America, and the fame
concern for their welfare, that they muft have
had for that part of the inhabitants of Britain who
fend no reprefentatives to parliament; and therefore I never thought the analogy between the ftate
of America, and trading towns in this ifland un-
reprefented, fo exact as to fatisfy the mind of any
man impartially bent upon juftice. But ftill taxation by parliament was the only legal, acknow-
ledged method of levying money through the
dominions of Britain; and if it involved peculiar

C   hard-

hardſhips when extended to America, were miniſtry to be blamed for purſuing it ? But what then
was to be done in this ſituation ? Was there no
remedy ? Muſt miniſtry inſiſt upon taxing America by act of Britiſh parliament, or muſt America ſubmit, though aware of conſequences de--
ſtructive of the freedom and proſperity of their
country ? Common ſenſe will at once ſuggeſt,
that as there is a very great difference between
exacting and carrying into effect laws which already exiſt, though they may be prejudicial to
the intereſt of the ſubject, and propoſing to enact
new laws of the ſame tendency, ſo they ought to
be oppoſed upon different principles, and by different methods. In the firſt caſe ſuppoſed, that
is, when miniſtry form their meaſures upon laws
already exiſting, no reflection ought to be thrown
out againſt them ; nay, perhaps they may deſerve
praiſe for greater firmneſs and fidelity in the diſcharge of their duty, and redreſs ought to be
ſought in time to come, by a reſpectful application
to the ſupreme legiſlative body of the nation.
But in the other caſe ſuppoſed, odium ought juſtly to fall upon thoſe who could have the wick-
edneſs to propoſe any new law manifeſtly founded
upon injuſtice, and deſtructive of the welfare of
any ſet of men. At the ſame time, if in ſuch a
caſe remonſtrances, and more peaceable plans of
reſiſtance, ſhould fail of ſucceſs, the firſt principles
of human nature would juſtify the boldeſt meaſures, in order to avert the dreaded miſchief.
This reaſoning will apply to the diſpute between
Britain and her Colonies. If the taxation of
America was admitted as neceſſary and juſt—if it
behoved the miniſters and parliament to follow
the ordinary and conſtitutional plan of exacting
                                              it—

it—if this method was found, or apprehended to
be productive, of peculiar danger when extended
to America, remonftrances and petitions ought
not only to have been prefented, but fome other
plan foberly propofed more fafe for America, and
equally effectual to procure that aid which Britain juftly demanded. Could ever America be
juftified for drawing the fword till fuch a plan had
been propofed and rejected?* It has not been
attended to, that grievances growing out of the
conftitution, or which follow from a minifter's
purfuing meafures in conformity to the conftitution, are to be confidered in a very different light
from thofe grievances which fpring from innovation, or a change of the eftablifhed laws, cuftoms
and government of a country. And it ought to
be carefully remembered, that miniftry did not
frame new acts of parliament to pave the way for
the taxation of America—they raifed their fyftem
upon acts of parliament already in being, and upon the principles of the law as it then ftood. †

C 2　　　　　　　　No

---

* It may be faid, that terms of accommodation were propofed by Congrefs in the petition to the King, brought over
and delivered by Mr. Penn. To fay nothing of the illegality
of that affembly, and the affront which the King and Parliament muft have incurred if they had treated with them, I afk
if this petition admits the power of parliament to tax America,
or implies confent to taxation in any fhape, or propofes to fub-
ftitute any plan to contribute to the fupplies of Britain ?

† The right of the Britifh parliament to tax her Colonies,
was not fo much as called in queftion in the Houfe of Commons
in the great debate upon American affairs, [Jan. 14. 1766.]
for the declaratory ftatute was carried without a divifion. The
fame fentiments feem to have been retained by oppofition at a
later period. March 5, 1770, it was propofed by Lord North
to repeal fo much of an act paffed the feventh of his prefent
Majefty, as related to impofing a tax upon paper painters colours,

No government upon earth can be so perfectly modelled, as not to admit occasionally of certain inconveniences and grievances. Nay, laws originally formed upon the wisest and most equitable construction, may, from a change of interests and circumstances, give a sanction to the violation of those rights which they were destined to protect and secure. When equity and justice require that such laws should be corrected or changed, wisdom will direct that it ought to be done with temper and reverence for the constitution. Exaggerated representations of constitutional grievances, or grievances which grow of the constitution; illiberal abuse of government, and violent and precipitate plans of redress, only tend to lay in ruins that fabric, which a small degree of expence and labour, skilfully directed, might repair and embellish. The opposition to the American tax, as conducted not only by the Americans, but by their friends in England, and levelled at the authority of parliament, had too much the shape of an assault upon the constitution itself.

The

lours and glass exported to the Colonies; but that the tax upon the tea, laid on by the same act, should still be continued, lest they should be thought to give way to American ideas, and to take away the other impositions, as having been contrary to the rights of the Colonies. It was answered by opposition, that this was an argument totally futile and ridiculous, because the right of Britain to tax the Colonies was sufficiently ascertained by two positive laws declaratory of that right, as well as by other taxes still existing in exercise of it.

"When Lord Chatham affirms, that the authority of the British parliament is not supreme over the Colonies, in the same sense in which it is supreme over Britain, I listen to him with diffidence and respect, but without the smallest conviction or assent." These are the words of Junius, a great admirer of Lord Chatham, introduced with this observation—That we are not to expect perfection in any man. [See Junius's Letter, October 5, 1771.]

The expediency of taxing America may ftill be objected to by thofe who allow, that the plan was not inconfiftent either with law or juftice. The oppofition it was to meet with, and all the dreadful effects which have enfued, fince the commencement of the unhappy war, were forefeen and foretold by more difcerning politicians, and were irrefiftible arguments for diffenting from the minifterial plan of taxing America. I think I may venture to affirm, that there is not a man in or out of adminiftration, who would have moved to impofe a tax upon America, if he had certainly forefeen the fatal confequences which it has produced. And this is one confiderable advantage of argument upon the fide of thofe who originally oppofed the American war, that they now appeal to events which correfpond exactly with their predictions and warnings. It is certain, that the opinion of the world muft, in a very confiderable degree, be affected by fuccefs. Suppofe any plan to have been formed, with as much wifdom and fkill as human genius ever poffeffed, yet if it has mifcarried in the iffue, either from mifconduct or mifchance, over which the author had no power, he will not be exempted from that cenfure which, in ftrict juftice, is due only to rafhnefs and folly. I fhall not now enter into a comparative view of the wealth, the refources, and the military force of Great-Britain and America—I fhall only fubmit a few plain confiderations to the judgment of the candid part of the nation who think for themfelves, and have not yet refigned their underftanding to the arbitrary dictates of any party.

Admitting the claims of Britain upon America to have been as juft, and our fuperiority as clear, as was held forth by the friends of adminiftration,

yet

yet have not a variety of circumſtances occurred
in the progreſs of this diſpute, to diminiſh the
power and cramp the exertions of Britain, and to
animate the courage and increaſe the ſtrength of
the rebellious Colonies? Has not the language of
oppoſition from the beginning, been one continued vindication of American rebellion? Nay,
have not encomiums and panegyrics upon rebellious generals, without a bluſh, been loudly
founded in both houſes of parliament? * Was not
the inability of Britain to prevail againſt America,
aſſerted by thoſe who were ſuppoſed to be beſt
acquainted

* A celebrated orator expatiated in the Houſe of Commons,
with tears, on the virtues of General Montgomery, who fell at
the head of the rebel army before Quebec. I am confident,
that there is not a man in this nation, more diſpoſed than the
Author of theſe Obſervations, to make allowance for the influence of prejudice, and to give credit for virtue and principle,
to men of different parties and ſentiments in religion and poli-
tics. Suppoſe it ſhould be admitted, that a man who had been
born in Britain, and who had taken the oaths of allegiance to
his preſent Majeſty, and ſubſiſted by ſerving him in the capacity of a ſoldier—ſuppoſe it ſhould be admitted, that ſuch a man,
through miſinformation or miſconſtruction of the deſigns of government, might, without any ſtain upon his virtue or patriotiſm, join with thoſe who ſeek to deſtroy the intereſt or government of his native country, yet it is neither prudent or
generous to make a public declaration of ſuch ſentiments. Do
they not ſeem to disjoin the ideas of morality and patriotiſm?
Do they not authorize latitudinarian ſentiments concerning the
attachment and duties which men owe their country? Do they
not diſcourage the hopes of thoſe, who ſeek for honour by ſteady
perſeverance in the plain path of loyalty, at the hazard of life
and fortune? There were unqueſtionably in the number of thoſe
who were deluded by attachment to the family of Stewart, and
who fell in their cauſe in the years 1715 and 1745, men of
integrity and honour—but would it have been ſeaſonable, de-
cent, or lawful, to have given any advantage to ſuch men, by
exalting their reputation at a time when they were in arms
againſt the family ſeated upon the throne, upon whoſe eſtabliſh-
ment all our moſt valuable rights and privileges depend?

acquainted with the strength, and most attached
to the honour, of the nation. What might have
been naturally expected from such conduct, has
actually come to pass. The speeches of members
in opposition quickly wafted over the Atlantic,
and repeated in strains still more exaggerated and
emphatic, have given a double advantage to our
enemies, by nourishing their hopes, and depressing
the courage and resolution of the friends of Britain. I make no doubt, but that thousands in
America resisted the demands of government,
prompted by the pure influence of principle, and
an apprehension of the danger which, as they be-
lieved, threatened their liberties—but still, in the
most candid construction, I am persuaded, that a
far greater proportion were drawn into rebellion
by an immediate regard to their own personal
interest and safety. Now, considering the divided,
embarrassed state of British councils, and reckoning merely upon chances, did not every motive
of immediate interest and safety draw to the side
of rebellion? The insults and depredations of
mobs were certainly avoided—a change of ministry, no improbable event, might entirely reverse
the state of things, render abortive the threats
and preparations of Britain, and make the worse
the better cause. At any rate, should these expectations be frustrated, and should the cause upon
which prove unsuccessful, from the number and
influence of their partisans, and the distinguished
lenity of the nation and Prince whom they had
offended, an indemnity might certainly be expected, together with the speedy re-establishment of
that peace and order which they had imprudently
violated. Nothing but perfect unanimity in the
British councils, and determined vigour and ex-

pedition, could difcourage a ftrain of reafoning fo obvious and juft, and prevent that fatal ftubbornnefs of rebellion which it has confirmed. Let us fuppofe, that oppofition in parliament had purfued a different fyftem of conduct—that at the commencement of the difcontents of America, they had employed all their zeal and influence to perfuade her to fubmit her grievances and wrongs to a parliamentary difcuffion—fuppofe they had advifed fuch conceffions as could not, in any view, have expofed her liberties to danger—and fuppofe they had added threats to perfuafions, and inftead of depreciating, had employed the eloquence by which many of them are diftinguifhed, to exhibit a fair view of the claims of the Mother Country, and the refources of which fhe was poffeffed. Can it admit of any queftion, whether, by fuch a tenor of conduct, they would not have obtained for America all the terms fhe could have demanded, confiftently with law and juftice, and ftopped that torrent of blood which has almoft exhaufted the ftrength of the fathers and the children? Then fhould the bleffing of the peacemaker have refted upon their heads, and generations to come fhould have called them bleffed.

But let us reverfe the picture—America has declared herfelf independent upon Britain—fhe has renounced the parent who gave her exiftence, and nourifhed her in her helplefs years with a mother's tendernefs—fhe has courted the alliance of that very power who fought her deftruction, and from which fhe was fo lately faved by an immenfe profufion of the treafure and the blood of Britain. The intereft of America and France are now infeparably interwoven. Is it poffible, that a mind infpired with juft, moral ideas, can contemplate
the

the conduct of America without a lively fenfe of indignation and abhorrence? The man who can behold filial ingratitude with indifference, muft himfelf be deeply infected with the turpitude of guilt. Is there a fon of Britain fo abject, as not to be moved by the infults and wrongs which have been heaped upon the parent ftate? To compleat thy infamy, O Britain! America independent, America leagued with the Houfe of Bourbon— (alarming, difgraceful founds!)—America ftill finds patrons and advocates among the patriots of modern days!—I could wifh at this moment, O Chatham, to bury in eternal oblivion the errors and caprice of the man, whilft I recollect the hero burfting the fetters of difeafe and infirmity, and flafhing indignation and fury upon that fpurious fon of Britain, who had the effrontery to name with approbation the independence of America. * In a domeftic quarrel, when the neareft relations have fallen out with one another, nothing is more common than for the inveterate enemies of the family, with diabolical officioufnefs, to blow the flames of difcord, in order to widen the breach, and to involve parents and children in the fame common difgrace and mifery. At fome happy moment of coolnefs and reflection, the voice of nature, though long fuppreffed, is again liftened to with refpect, the powers of affection refume their wonted authority, a reconciliation takes place, the arts of incendiaries are detected, and by the parents and children they are ever after held in abhorrence. May fuch finally be the fuccefs and the reward of the abettors of the American rebellion!

But

* The Duke of Richmond, the moft unwearied opponent of adminiftration.

But it may be enquired, Does the whole burden of guilt reft upon the head of members of parliament in oppofition? Are the calamities and prolongation of the American war, to be imputed entirely to the encouragement which they have given to our enemies, and the obftructions which they have thrown in the way of our fchemes and operations of war? Was it even in their power to perpetrate the worft purpofes of their heart, without the concurrence, or at leaft the indolence and timidity of adminiftration? Truth, and not the favour of any party, is the object of this Enquiry. It is impoffible for the warmeft advocates of miniftry, to cover them altogether from the charge of mifconduct, in the different ftages of the difpute between Britain and America, Some of their moft glaring errors I fhall now fpecify. And becaufe there is nothing mor' -afy than to be wife after experiment, and to tel ..uw that might have been done better, which wu have actually feen to have been done wrong, I fhall confine myfelf to fuch inftances of mifconduct as were obvious, and condemned by many of the moft impartial and penetrating, at the very ti ne they were propofed.

Miniftry, from the beginning of the American difturbances, have difcovered a timidity and delay which have given great advantage to our enemies. In every part of America, and particularly at Bofton, the fervants of government were infulted, and the orders of government treated with contempt. Mobs every day became more frequent and formidable, and were acquiring entire afcendancy over the minds of the people—the bands of government were broken. Could it admit of a moment's hefitation, whether the feafon was not arrived when it would have been expedient to difplay,

play, at leaft in one inftance, a vigorous exertion
of legal power? The people form their judgment
of the force and dignity of government, from what
falls immediately under their notice and experience. From the tinge and quality of the ftream,
we judge of the fountain from which it iffues.
The feeblenefs and remiffnefs of magiftrates, naturally infufe into the minds of the people a contempt of the head from which their authority is
derived—from contempt, the tranfition to refift-
ance and open rebellion is fhort and eafy.

The firft effectual intimation of the difpleafure
of Britain, was by the enactment of the Bofton
port bill. * The operation of this to the difad-
vantage of the trade of New-England was more
remote, whilft its effect in irritating the paffions
of the people was immediate and powerful. If
you inflame the rage of an angry man, without
curbing his power, you only increafe the danger
to which you ftand expofed. When a multitude
have combined againft the eftablifhed government,
they lofe fight of more diftant intereft, and defpife
every threat and intimation of difpleafure that
does not immediately reach their perfons. Thus
the Bofton port bill operated rather to inflame
than appeafe the difaffection of America, whilft
it did not in any degree diminifh their force, or
interrupt their preparations, to fhake off depend-
ance upon the Mother Country.

Not lefs unfortunate was the next meafure purfued by adminiftration, in order to prevent the
extremity

* A bill paffed the Houfe of Commons, March 24, and received the royal affent the 31ft, 1774, to difcontinue the land-
ing, difcharging, lading and fhipping of goods and merchan-
dize at the town and within the harbour of Bofton in Maffa-
chufett's-Bay.

extremity of proceeding to hoftilities againft America. It was propofed in February, 1774, that if any one of the provinces fhould make provifion, or contribute to government, according to their refpective condition, they fhould be confidered as returning to their allegiance, and be taken into the King's peace.* To mingle rigour with lenity in a due proportion—to difcern the precife point at which conceffions ought to end, and force begin, is perhaps one of the rareft and moft important accomplifhments of a politician—for as, upon the one hand, a reafonable and prudent condefcenfion to the prejudices and defires of the people, may nip the buds of difcontent, and avert thofe civil commotions, which give the deepeft wounds to the profperity of a nation—fo, on the other hand, there is a certain crifis in the humours and paffions of men, after which all conceffions and milder plans of reconciliation are conftrued into weaknefs and fear, and increafe that temerity and turbulence which they were intended to mollify and compofe. There were, I believe, very few perfons unbiaffed by the prejudice and influence of party, and acquainted with the hiftory of fimilar events, who could doubt whether conciliatory meafures or force ought to have been employed by Britain, at the period to which

---

* February 1775, it was moved by Lord North, that when the Governor, Council, Affembly, or General Court of any of his Majefty's provinces, fhall make provifion, according to their refpective conditions, for contributing their proportion to the common defence, fuch proportion to be raifed under the authority of the General Court or General Affembly, and difpofable by parliament, it will be proper, if fuch propofal fhall be approved of by his Majefty in parliament, to forbear, in refpect of fuch province, to levy any duty, tax or affeffment, or to impofe any further duty, tax or affeffment.

which I now refer. The conciliatory bill, pro-
posed in February, 1774, as might have been
expected, instead of reclaiming a single province,
only served to diffuse over the whole empire an
impression of the fluctuation of ministry, to shake
the confidence of friends, to raise the hopes of
enemies, and extend their opportunity of provid-
ing materials for waging war against the Mother
Country—but treaties of peace have fallen to the
ground—the trumpet of war is sounded—the
sword is drawn—and now do dispatch and activity
atone for past neglect, irresolution and delay?
Which leads me to mark the errors of administration at a more advanced period of this civil war.

The employing foreign troops was a measure
liable to many exceptions, and has been proba-
bly, in part, the occasion of retarding the success
of ministry in terminating the American disturbances. I do not intend to enlarge upon those
common place arguments, which I think evince
the ill policy of resorting to the protection of
mercenary troops, in any case where unavoidable
necessity does not require it. In a civil war, peculiar reasons aggravate the impropriety and danger of such a measure. Does it not convey to
rebellious subjects an impression of the weakness
and the fears of government, when it cannot rely
upon its own internal strength and resources to
enforce the measures which it has directed? Does
it not irritate the resentment of misguided and
undutiful subjects, to be in danger of falling by
the hands of those against whom they have committed no offence, and who have no natural and
original interest in the dispute in which they are
engaged? Does it not teach an evil lesson against
ourselves, and inculcate upon our revolted subjects
the

the juftice and neceffity of retaliating, by reforting to foreign fupport and affiftance? Has it not been actually pleaded by the Americans, as the motive of foliciting an alliance with the ancient and natural enemies of Britain? Is it not in the reafon of the thing to be expected, that mercenary troops, who have neither from prejudice nor intereft any attachment to the power who has hired them, may be eafily debauched, and prevailed upon by more immediate and extenfive gain, to turn the fword againft thofe on whofe behalf it was firft drawn? Does not fuch a meafure deprefs the fpirits of the people at home, and weaken the reputation of the nation abroad? Has not the number of regiments levied with fuch expedition in every part of Britain, during the laft three years of the war, fully demonftrated that the nation was poffeffed of ample internal force, and by no means reduced to the neceffity of opening campaigns in America, with fuch a proportion of foreign and mercenary allies? If the fame exertion had been made at the beginning of thefe difturbances—if the fame ardour and fuccefs in augmenting our army and navy with Britifh fubjects had been encouraged by adminiftration, it might have overawed rebellion, and perhaps prevented even the occafion of expofing our numerous troops to action.

If the incapacity or mifconduct of thofe who are employed in the executive departments, juftly lie at the door of the perfons who have appointed them, never fince the exiftence of the Britifh nation did any minifter ftand under fuch an accumulated load of guilt. Will the moft zealous advocates for the prefent adminiftration deny, that they have been miftaken or unfortunate in the choice of the Generals and Admirals to whom the moft

moſt important commands have been entruſted.
There are ſome facts which carry in their face
ſuch palpable evidence, that it is impoſſible the
higheſt authority, or the teſtimony of ten thouſand
witneſſes, can either ſtrengthen or diminiſh the
belief of the man who has been made acquainted
with them—if ever any fact fell under this deſcrip-
tion, it is that to which our attention is at preſent
directed. Is there any perſon of reflection in this
kingdom, who ſtill remains in doubt with reſpect
to the behaviour of Sir William Howe? Is it poſ-
ſible that his perſonal aſſurance, or the teſtimony
of his fellow officers, or their pompous celebra-
tion of his victories at Philadelphia, or the reſult
of the enquiry in the Houſe of Commons, can
now convince any man that Sir William Howe
acquitted himſelf in the American command as a
wiſe and brave General, or as a Friend to Britain?
Nay, I appeal to thoſe who are conſcious to themſelves of having been originally prepoſſeſſed with
the ſtrongeſt prejudices in his favour, (of which
number I confeſs myſelf to have been one) whether, in a ſingle inſtance, their expectations have
been anſwered? From the opening of the war,
has not his reputation been in a gradual decline,
till at laſt he has ſunk into the moſt debaſed ſtate
of national odium and neglect? Suppoſe your
prejudices for the General to have been ſo ſtrong,
as to have made you confide in him, notwith-
ſtanding his retreat from a conquered enemy on
Long-Iſland, fully ſatisfied, that it was more
prudent to attack the adverſary by regular approaches—if you could have been perſuaded that
the flight of ten thouſand men, obſtructed by a
dangerous ferry, could have been accompliſhed
without any reflection upon the vigilance of the
Gene-

General—if you could ftill have been fo diffident of your own judgment, as to have admitted im-plicitly of the propriety of lingering at New-York, whilft the enemy, who had abandoned it, were occupied in fortifying themfelves at White Plains ; after all this, could you with patience liften to any man, who fhould endeavour to perfuade you that fixteen thoufand men, flufhed with victory, ought again to have been reftrained from falling upon a panic-ftruck army, whofe numbers were fo much ir ´ rior to thofe of their conquerors? Could you calmly attend to any vindication of the General's conduct in embarking his troops, and expofing them to the dangers of a tedious voyage, when they might with greater fafety have been conducted by land to the place of deftination, or when they ought to have been employed in fe-conding the operations of Burgoyne's army, who, trufting to their affiftan'ce, had ventured into the moft dangerous paffes of the enemy's country? To the man who would ftill contend for the repu-tation of Sir William Howe, would you not re-ply—This is an infult to my underftanding—my confidence is exhaufted—I have hitherto been ftruggling againft conviction—I have been a dupe to my own credulity and prepoffeffions for the wifdom of the miniftry, and fkill of the General—but now, feeling has at once reftored my reafon, and roufed my indignation—the difgrace of my country covers me with fhame—the injured ho-nour of Britain touches my inmoft foul. How art thou fallen, O thou who wert fo great before !—Where is thy fpirit, O Britain! Why does not indignation pervade every heart? Why did not miniftry for once forget their fears? Why did not oppofition forget their refentmenss? Why

did

did not the people, with one voice, demand vengeance upon the man who had degraded the honour of the nation, and plunged her into the loweſt abyſs of calamity and diſgrace I If America ſhall be loſt to Britain, it is not the wiſdom of a Congreſs, the generalſhip of a Waſhington, nor the numbers nor the bravery of the troops that he commanded, which have effected it. Generations to come ſhall, in the bitterneſs of their ſoul, execrate the memory of the man who by ignorance, diſſipation, rapacioufneſs and treachery, protracted the period of gain and diſtinction to himſelf, and ſported away the blood and treaſures of his country I

The appointment of Admiral Keppel to the command of the fleet, might, perhaps with propriety, be adduced as another evidence of the imprudence and ignorance which miniſtry have diſcovered in the choice of their ſervants. In this inſtance, indeed, a greater latitude of opinion may, in candour, be allowed. With ſuperior force he engaged the French fleet, diſcontinued the engagement, or withdrew from it, though he affirmed that he had ſoundly beaten them. He declined to purſue the enemy's fleet upon a lee ſhore, that is, whilſt he was not more t' an ninety or an hundred miles from land. He has been tried by a court-martial and acquitted, received the thanks of both houſes of parliament, and the applauſe of many mobs. Sir Hugh Palliſer, the ſuppoſed cauſe of diſappointing the Admiral's expectations of utterly deſtroying the French fleet, has been alſo tried and acquitted. Many think it difficult to reconcile theſe two deciſions. The enemies of Admiral Keppel boldly aſſert, that he did not do all he might have done to deſtroy the

D

French

French fleet. His friends muft in fecret regret, that however inconteftible the latent accomplifhments of the hero, and however unblameable his conduct upon the 27th of July, 1778, his fuccefs was but of little moment. The impartial part of mankind will obferve, that the Admiral has rather been overpaid with applaufe, that a more liberal proportion of it could not have fallen to his fhare if he had utterly exterminated the French fleet, and that it would have been both modeft and manly, to have referved fome part of it for deeds of uncontroverted fuccefs, and fubftantial fervice, rendered to his country.

The mifconduct of Generals and Admirals, though in the firft inftance it draws difgrace and indignation upon their own heads, muft finally redound to the reproach and condemnation of the miniftry who employ them. In vain does the moft profound wifdom refide in the cabinet—in vain are the beft meafures concerted and adopted there, if penetration is wanting to difcover the correfponding talents which are neceffary to perform and carry them into effect. The great genius of Lord Chatham, was in nothing more confpicuous than in that fagacity with which he penetrated into the talents and characters of men, with invariable fuccefs felecting thofe who were moft likely to excel in the feveral departments to which he affigned them—and I do not mean to detract from his merit when I add, that this was perhaps the principal caufe of the amazing victories and brilliant profperity, which fignalized his adminiftration.

In defence of the conduct of our prefent minifters it has been pleaded, that at a period of emergency, which required the moft intimate and cordial
dial

dial union at home, they did well to purfue heal-
ing meafures; and in order to convert and divide
oppofition, what plan more fpecious, than to
commit the moft critical operations of the war to
Generals and Admirals who were connected with
it. I am not, in general, difpofed to think well
either of the wifdom or honour of that policy,
which poftpones the intereft of friends, in order
to weaken and defeat the intrigues of enemies—
but I oppofe argument as well as feeling to this
favourite plan, of calling out the retainers to an
oppofite faction, to command armies and fleets
which were to engage in expeditions, of which
they profeffed to difapprove upon principle.
Might it not have been forefeen, that the mifconduct or misfortune of fuch men, would furnifh
oppofition with new arguments in fupport of the
opinions which they had announced from the beginning of thefe difturbances? If fuccefs fhould
not crown the attempt of Generals, who, by the
teftimony of all parties, were the moft deferving
of truft, and of whofe abilities minifters efpecially
muft have been convinced, (fince no other motive
could be affigned for employing them) if under
them American rebellion grew more obftinate and
rancorous, the caufe was defperate, and the farther profecution of it vain and ruinous. The
friends of oppofition had not the fame motives to
prompt them to a circumfpect and vigorous exertion, which muft have influenced the friends of
miniftry; and if they really could have had the
iniquity to betray their country, they might have
done it without an equal hazard of cenfure and
difgrace. The conduct of Generals and Admirals
in the intereft of miniftry, would have been dili-
gently enquired into—operations conducted by

them

them would have been watched with a jealous eye—every inftance of bad fuccefs examined with the fevereft fcrutiny, and actual mifconduct fet forth in fuch colours, as to have drawn on them the certain vengeance of the nation. Under the confcioufnefs of guilt no hope of mercy could have been entertained. But fuppofe neither the abilities nor the integrity of Generals and Admirals, who have been employed by miniftry, could have been called in queftion, were cordial obedience and bold exertions, to be expected from men whofe minds were warped by connections in a different intereft, and who, from the habit of oppofition, had been inured to controvert and defpife the fentiments of thofe from whom they were to receive their orders? When a fenfe of gratitude and zeal for the honour of a benefactor, co-operate with principles and regard to the public welfare, there is ground to expect the richeft fruits of genius and abilities. The critical juncture of affairs required a combination of all thofe qualities, which, in the ordinary courfe of things, infure the fidelity, vigour and fuccefs, of thofe who led forth the armies and fleets of Britain. To the imprudent choice of minifters, in preferring the friends of oppofition to the moft important trufts in the executive department, we have good reafon to afcribe fome of the moft difcouraging circumftances which occur in the prefent ftate of the nation. Diffipation, trifling, and treachery, have been vindicated—retreats and fruitlefs rencounters have got the name and the praife of victory—the ftandard of national valour has been lowered—the multitud- have fhouted—the fober part of the nation have been conftrained to acquiefce in the ridiculous and farcical triumphs.

But

But in no inſtance has the conduct of adminiſtration been more juſtly liable to cenſure, than
in the language they held, and the meaſures they
purſued, at a more advanced period of the war,
after the unfortunate campaign of 1777. Every
one may well remember the effects which the total overthrow of Burgoyne's army, and the timid,
wavering operations, and ſmall amount of the
ſucceſs of General Howe, produced upon the nation at home. Every man felt, as for himſelf,
the indignity and reproach which his country had
ſuſtained. A ſpirit of reſentment run through the
great body of the people. America had hitherto
been attacked upon the formal reſolutions of men
in office, and with a caution which damped the
ſpirits, and cramped the hands of thoſe very men
who were employed to carry them into execution.
But now national honour, national reſentment,
every principle that produces the moſt ſtrenuous
efforts, atchieves the moſt glorious exploits, and
elevates individuals and ſocieties above all the
calculations of natural ſtrength and reſources,
were bent upon the humiliation of Ameri   and
promiſed certain and ſpeedy redreſs of the aﬀronts
and injuries we had ſuſtained. Subſcriptions were
in every corner opened for levying troops—a
martial ſpirit ſprung up—the whole nation ſeemed
ardent to ruſh into battle. Here was preſented
to miniſtry a propitious opportunity for purſuing
meaſures, bold, ſpirited and deciſive. What
might they not have accompliſhed, had they che-
riſhed the ſpirit of the nation, and afforded it
ſcope and opportunity for action? Are not the
higheſt efforts of national fortitude, rouſed by
preceding examples of diſaſter and reproach? Did
ever the braveſt nation in the world appear more

brave,

brave, than in thofe exertions by which they rofe
again from the loweft ebb of bad fortune, and
repaid their conquerors with deftruction? The
repulfe of Hannibal after the battle of Cannæ,
brought more honour to the General and the army,
than the moft extenfive conquefts which the Roman ftate attained in the career of her profperity.
The fluggifhnefs and defpondency which overwhelmed this nation at the beginning of the late
war, contributed to render the period that follows
the moft interefting and glorious that adorns the
annals of Britain. Did miniftry avail themfelves
of thefe arguments and examples ? The ardour of
the nation was quenched—the language of timidity was again adopted, and a conciliatory bill upon
terms the moft humiliating to Britain was propofed. The propriety of that meafure let its re-
ception teftify. There is not an individual who
retains the fmalleft fpark of national honour, who
does not trace the deepeft affront to the plan of
conciliation, which was propofed by miniftry,
adopted with the unanimous confent of both
Houfes of Parliament, and rejected by the American Congrefs with difdain. After all, in juftice
to adminiftration, we ought to obferve, that even
their very errors are, in fome meafure, to be imputed to the obftinacy and contention of oppofition, which, during the whole progrefs of the
war, has clogged and thwarted the operations of
government. Some of the moft exceptionable
meafures, fuch as the conciliatory bill, have been
actually embraced in the way of compromife with
minority, in order to attain (what from late experience has appeared a vain expectation) the
concurrence of all parties to reftore their country,
reduced to the loweft extremity by domeftic quar-
rels

rels and difputes. Nor is it fo eafy a point, to
decide who the miniftry are. The body minifterial, like the matter of the animal fyftem, is in a
continual fluctuation, and liable to change. The
men who were in the cabinet at the time of pro-
pofing the American tax, have fome of them appeared in the moft violent oppofition to the war,
which was the confequence of their own meafures.
The refignation of an office, or the change of a
party, in one moment obliterates the remembrance
of paft tranfgreffions, and perfectly purifies the
foul. It is impoffible to conceive any two perfons
to differ more from each other, than the fame
man differs from himfelf, when he happens to be
in or out of power.

From what has occurred in the preceding pages,
it muft appear to every candid enquirer, that fo
far as the prefent diftrefs of this nation has been
occafioned by the errors and mifconduct of perfons
at home, neither miniftry nor oppofition have
been guiltlefs. At the fame time it cannot be
doubted, to which of thefe the greateft fhare of
guilt ought in juftice to be charged, and whether
there can be any reafonable ground to hope for
better fuccefs from a change of hands, and under
the management of men, who, becaufe they have
not been gratified with honours and office according to expectation, have exerted their utmoft influence, in conjunction with thofe who have
fought the deftruction of their country, and but
too fuccefsfully prevailed to aggravate and protract her fufferings. From fuch men can we expect that energy, capacity and virtue, which, under the bleffing of heaven, are neceffary to reco-
ver the honour and profperity of this nation?
Without any deviation from the ftricteft impar-

tiality

tiality and regard to truth, many circumftances might be alledged, to extenuate that fhare of blame which is placed to the account of miniftry. It is hardly poffible to conceive a fituation of public affairs more critical and perplexing, than that in which the fervants of government found themfelves involved at the commencement of the American war. From a feries of meafures (which whether wife or unwife is not to the prefent purpofe) purfued through preceding adminiftrations unconnected with one another, perhaps of oppofite interefts and parties, a difpute between the Mother Country and her Colonies grew to be mature for decifion. What was the minifter of the day to do? To recede was impoffible. To go forward dangerous. To make conceffions to America was only to poftpone the period of decifion. The queftion would recur in a more intricate fhape, and a fentence muft fooner or later be pronounced. To plunge into a civil war, drew after it a hideous train of calamities—accumulation of national debt—decline of trade—bankruptcies—alienations of the affections of fellow citizens and brothers—a large profufion of the moft precious blood of the nation. Was it matter of furprize, that a minifter in circumftances fo peculiarly delicate and trying, was perplexed, wavering, and fearful? Wherever he turned his eyes, difficulties and dangers ftarted to his view. In whatever refolution he was to fettle, he anticipated a world of reproach and oppofition. If it was in vain to expect to unite the fentiments and interefts of all the members of the ftate, was it not the more neceffary to leffen the number of divifions, and to weaken the power of oppofition? Is it matter of aftonifhment, that too anxious a

pro-

profecution of this plan has given rife to meafures
apparently feeble, fluctuating and inconfiftent. I
might offer to the confideration of the candid part
of my countrymen, virtues and qualifications
which ought not to be overlooked becaufe they
are found in a minifter. I do not think, that the
abilities of the perfon who now prefides at the
head of public affairs, would lofe in a comparifon
with thofe of the moft refpectable perfons who
ftand in oppofition to him. His private virtues,
which are not only an ornament but an effential
qualification to a public character, I might place
in contraft with theirs. I might compare his minifterial conduct with that of his predeceffors in
office. Was there ever a minifter who exercifed
greater moderation and temper, in replying to the
rudeft invectives of his opponents, or who was fo
little prone to exert his power in refenting abufe
and contradiction, or who was more difpofed to
give due weight to their arguments, and adopt,
by their fuggeftion, any meafure that really feemed
calculated for national advantage? Or, finally,
was there ever a minifter whofe integrity was lefs
fufpected? To confirm thefe obfervations I might
remark, that in the efteem of the moft judicious
part of the nation, he ftands as high as any minifter ever has done within the remembrance of the
prefent age; nor do I think that the odium of the
people runs with fuch violence againft him, as it
did againft fome of the very men who wifh to wreft
the power out of his hands, when they formerly
filled the feats of government.

With thefe obfervations I intended to have
clofed, believing that I had taken in every thing
that properly belonged to the fubject of this trea-
tife. The increafing power of the crown, has been
lately

lately enumerated in the lift of public grievances, and reprefented as a juft ground of national difcontent and jealoufy. The prepofition has been moved in the Houfe of Commons, and affented to by a majority of members. As in the number of thefe, there are found many names who are not underftood to be adherents to any party, and who have not voted with oppofition in other queftions which followed that motion, it is but fair to afcribe their opinion to conviction, and an unbiaffed regard to the fafety of the conftitution. A fubject of fuch moment deferves the attention of every man who is a friend to his country, and who wifhes to convey to others thofe fentiments which he is perfuaded are moft favourable to public good.

The influence of the crown may be enlarged or reftricted by the prevailing opinion and prejudices of the people, by an acceffion or diminution of thofe privileges which are underftood of right to belong to it, or by the temper and conduct of the Prince who fills the throne.

When the fentiments of the nation in general are favourable to monarchy, the Prince may not only act up to the plenitude of prerogative, but extend and ftretch his power beyond thofe ftrict limitations of law, to which he would not even dare to approach in an age of jealoufy and diftruft. The diftractions and miferies which overwhelmed Great-Britain after the fubverfion of the conftitution, under republican, or, more properly fpeaking, military government, ftill frefh in the memory of the people at the period of the reftoration, turned the tide of fentiment into an oppofite channel, and afforded Charles the Second advantages for the extenfion of prerogative, which,
happily

happily for us, his indolence and love of pleafure did not permit him to underftand and improve.

But though the people efpoufe fentiments unfavourable to monarchy, and are jealous and watchful againft every innovation upon the conftitution, yet from a variety of different incidents which fall out in the ftate of a nation, and again.... which it is impoffible that any laws can provide, a great acceffion of power may accrue to the prerogative of the crown. Conqueft, territorial acquifitions, and a neceffary increafe of offices, may throw an additional weight into the fcale of prerogative, though the Prince be not ambitious, nor the people remifs and deficient in zeal for liberty.

And again, though the prejudices of the people may be againft prerogative, and though no incidents may have happened in the ftate of a nation to increafe it, yet a Prince of immoderate ambition, and ordinary talents, may contrive many effectual plans, and avail himfelf of many occafional circumftances, to augment his power and circumfcribe the rights and privileges of his people. And here I muft obferve by the way, that as in a free ftate it is hardly poffible for the Prince to make any confiderable acquifition of power without the affections of his people, fo their liberties will never be in greater danger, nor will there be greater occafion of jealoufy, than at a feafon when a Prince courts popularity too much, and binds to vulgar humours and prejudices, however inconfiftent they may be with the folid advantage and intereft of the nation. * For the fame reafon

mini-

* Had his Majefty complied with the numerous petitions prefented to him in the years 1770 and 1771, to diffolve that parliament

minifters who ftand higheft in the good graces of the people, will be the moft proper inftruments to overturn the conftitution, and may, without lofs of efteem, eftablifh fuch precedents as may weaken, in future times, the fecurity of the fubject, and counteract the fpirit of our laws and conftitution. I might appeal to recent facts in confirmation of thefe remarks. Mr. Pitt, in the zenith of his popularity, iffued general warrants without hefitation, but who ever thought of calling into queftion the lawfulnefs of any meafure, purfued by the man who fo often and fo loudly had declaimed in the caufe of liberty and the conftitution.

liament which had expelled Mr. Wilkes, and fuftained Colonel Luttrell's election, and which had then exifted only two feffions ; or had he, in a later inftance, complied with the petition of the Admirals, December 1778, to prevent the trial of Admiral Keppel, he might, with an immediate acquifition of popularity to himfelf, have eftablifhed a precedent, which, in future time, would have been favourable to the extenfion of prerogative, and dangerous to the rights of the fubject.

Allow that the Houfe of Commons had done wrong, in fuftaining Colonel Luttrell's election, and excluding Mr. Wilkes, yet if his Majefty had applied the remedy pointed out, and diffolved the parliament, might not miniftry have availed themfelves of the precedent, to have got rid, by a premature extinction, of a future parliament which was not enough obfequious to the pleafure of the court. Or allowing that Admiral Keppel had been invidioufly accufed, and from this confideration his Majefty had been induced to avert, by the interpofition of prerogative, a trial, from which in that cafe the Admiral had nothing to fear, yet might not a fucceeding Prince, lefs a friend to juftice, have imitated the example in circumftances widely different, in order to fcreen from merited punifhment a favourite fervant, who had abufed his truft, and actually tarnifhed the honour of the Britifh flag.

Let any one who reads the hiftory of the late revolution in Sweden, foberly confider, whether the ftates could have been deprived of their privileges, and the kingdom of its liberty, if the popularity of the Prince had not been fo great, and the confidence of the people in him fo entire.

ftitution. The difpenfing power exercifed by the Prince, in lay' ; an embargo on fhips laden with corn, and prohibiting the exportation of it in October, 1766, was not only recommended to the Privy Council by Lord Camden, but defended afterwards in the Houfe of Peers, by arguments which have not been heard fince the reign of an arbitrary Prince. * But the very language which had grated Englifh ears, at a period when the nation was deeply infected with the principles of flavery, was heard, without refentment, from the man who had pronounced a fentence in favour of Mr. Wilkes.

Let us now apply thefe obfervations to the prefent times, and enquire how far any of the caufes
above

* November 24, 1766, a bill was brought in by a fervant of the crown, to indemnify all perfons who had acted in obedience to a late act of council, Sept. 26, 1766, laying an embargo upon fhips loaded with corn. Members in oppofition were not fatisfied with the terms of the bill, becaufe it did not fully exprefs the illegality of the meafure, and include thofe who had advifed it. The bill was therefore amended and extended to thofe who advifed, as well as to thofe who had acted in that meafure. When it was brought to the Houfe of Peers, to the aftonifhment of his old friends, Lord Camden, then Chancellor, who had formerly been the great champion for liberty, defended the late exertion of prerogative, not only from the peculiar circumftances which occafioned it, but as a matter of right. He contended, that the crown has a legal, inherent right, founded upon neceffity, to fufpend an act of the legiflature. He who had pronounced the deprivation of liberty for a fingle hour, an irreparable injury, faid, that if the late exertion of prerogative was tyranny, it was but forty days tyranny at the outfide. The dangerous tendency of this doctrine, and its exact conformity to that which had been pleaded as a vindication for the moft tyrannical practices of the Stuarts, was, with his peculiar perfpicuity of argument and energy of expreffion, defcribed by Lord Man-field, who, upon a calm review of all his councils and decifions, appears the wifeft and moft fteady friend to liberty and the conftitution.

above recited have already operated, or may be apprehended hereafter to operate, to the increase or diminution of the power of the crown.

With regard to the first of these, I think there can be hardly any occasion for adducing arguments to prove, that national prejudice does not now run upon the side of prerogative. It is, I think, a matter of fact glaring to every man who bestows the smallest attention upon the state of political affairs, which fall within the compass of his own experience. I appeal to the tenor of political publications, to the strain of free and ordinary conversation, and to the language and sentiments of confederated bodies of men of every denomination, and in every part of the kingdom. Can the most zealous friend to liberty, who adverts to these observations, pretend to suspect that she is losing ground in the affections of the people, or that the partisans of prerogative are increasing in numbers and influence. The political pamphlets with which the press has been daily teeming, since the period of the revolution, exceed all reckoning. Slavery and arbitrary power are terms which often occur, but it is only to render them black and detestable. Many warnings are given to guard against the incroachments of prerogative, and that just deference and respect which are due to the dignity of the first magistrate, have been often laid aside; but there is not, I believe, a single author, who has professedly espoused the opposite system, and either avowedly or indirectly asserted, that an increase of crown influence is desirable, or would prove beneficial to the nation. Nay, so enlarged and liberal are the sentiments of men upon the subjects of government, that if any author should in our day,

ever

ever fo remotely hint at thofe wild fentiments
concerning prerogative, which were current in
the laft century, he would be regarded as a fool
rather than a knave, and univerfal contempt would
prove a fufficient antidote againft the contagion
of his fentiments. I might appeal to the conftant,
uniform declaration of men of all different parties
and interefts, who compofe the great council of
the nation. Is there a man in or out of power,
Whig or Tory, who dares to exprefs a wifh for
the extenfion of prerogative, or are their deeds
inconfiftent with their words? Has any meafure
been contrived or carried into execution in this
reign, with the deliberate purpofe of throwing
additional influence into the hands of the Prince?
Nay, have not meafures evidently tending to circumfcribe his authority, been adopted without
oppofition from miniftry, though it may have
been doubtful how far they were agreeable to law,
and though they were manifeftly contrary to precedent? I might refer to the uniform complexion
of decifion in all our courts of juftice. Is it not a
received maxim, that in every inftance where the
intereft of the crown and the fubject come into
competition, and where any room for doubt remains either in point of law or evidence, that the
intereft of the latter ought to be preferred? I
might more minutely examine the fentiments declared by corporate bodies, and all voluntary
affemblies and affociations of the people in every
part of the nation. Is there not an evident lean-
ing or bias to liberty? Is there not a jealoufy of
the influence of the Prince? Is there not a prone-
nefs to fufpect the immediate fervants of government? I might appeal to the voice of promifcu-
ous focieties; and with regard to any collective
body

body or company of men accidentally brought together, I might lay odds upon the conjecture, that their fuffrages, if gathered, would come out in favour of libeity and the conftitution. To corroborate thefe obfervations I might add, that the conduct of the Houfe of Commons upon the 6th of April was a refutation of the doctrine which the majority maintained, and the refult of the vote eftablifhed a matter of fact in oppofition to a fpeculative propofition, which it had taken for granted. ·

But in the fecond place it may be enquired, how far the power of the crown has increafed from accidental caufes? Has not the extenfion of territory, attended with the multiplication of offices, unavoidably increafed the number and wealth of retainers to the crown? Are not new channels of expectation opened, which have a diffufive influence in attracting homage and obfequioufnefs to the will of the great perfonage from whom fuccefs and gratification muft flow? Is there not good reafon to apprehend danger from this quarter? The danger is already apprehended. The fears of men are in full proportion to the danger. Inftead of inflaming thefe to a greater degree, it is the duty of every one who wifhes to maintain the conftitution pure and entire, to reftrain them within the bounds of reafon, and to mark out fuch a plan of exertion as may equally prevent the encroachments of prerogative, and thofe violent ftruggles of faction, which are equally ruinous to the peace and liberty of the fubject.

Whilft the revenue of the crown depends entirely upon the Commons or people, it is hardly poffible that the Prince can aim at any violent ftretch of power, or attempt to carry into execution

tion any meafure hurtful to his people, or even difagreeable to their inclinations. It will therefore be the object of every true patriot, to preferve this conftitutional dependence, and to oppofe every meafure calculated to eftablifh a fixed, independent revenue upon the Prince. As the executive part of government is lodged entirely in the hands of the crown, a confiderable degree of influence is neceffary to gain that concurrence, and produce that vigour, which are effential to the fuccefs of public meafures. But it cannot be denied, that the influence of the crown arifes, in a great meafure, from the difpofal of offices; and in this light it deferves attention, how far it is confiftent with the true intereft of the nation, to reduce the number and emoluments of office; that is, whether danger may not arife to the conftitution by reducing the influence of the crown fo far, as to impair that vigour which is neceffary to the fuccefsful exertion of the executive part of government. It is indeed difficult to draw the line, or to fix with precifion the boundaries where the influence of the crown ought to ftop. In an age when either the prejudices of the people, or the temper of the Prince, tend towards prerogative, a true patriot will wifh to go as far as he can in an oppofite direction, without wounding the conftitution, or infringing the eftablifhed laws of his country. If the creation of new offices be an uncontroverted addition to the influence of the crown, the good of the conftitution certainly requires, that fuch power fhould never be exerted but upon neceffary occafions, and when the important bufinefs of the nation indifpenfibly requires it. If any plan had been purfued to annex bufinefs to finecure offices, or to devolve the increaf-

E

ing

ing bufinefs of government upon thofe perfons, who are not required to give any returns of thought or labour for the emoluments which they already enjoy, I believe there would have been little occafion to have added to the burden of the nation, or the power of the crown, by the creation of new offices. It would refleft immortal honour on the prefent minifter, if he would exert thofe talents with which he is fo liberally endowed, in framing and digefting fuch a plan as might be effeftual to prevent either the increafe of new offices, or the growing expence of thofe which already exift. Notwithftanding the obloquy of thofe who envy his power, there are thoufands of the beft friends to the conftitution, who look up to him not only as the moft able, but as the moft difpofed to correft mifmanagement, to forward fchemes of real œconomy and ufefulnefs, and eftablifh the lafting profperity of his country. The fecret influence of the crown is always more to be dreaded than that which is open and vifible. Men who bear the names of public offices, or who avowedly accept, of penfions, muft ever be more reftrained by a regard to charafter, than thofe who derive emolument from the fame fource in a fuppreffed and concealed way. The very fufpicion and diftruft which the people entertain of the fervants of the crown, has an influence in deterring them from the fupport of any meafure which is notorioufly violent or illegal. The Prince himfelf would not efcape the fevereft cenfure, were he to difmifs a minifter from his office, or withdraw from a member of either houfe his penfion, for no other reafon but becaufe he had re-fufed to give his fupport to any meafure which appeared to him arbitrary, or fubverfive of the

con-

conftitution, and deftructive of the intereft of the
nation—but over fecret, concealed penfioners, the
public have no fuch awe or reftraint—they may
profefs principle when they are moved by intereft
—the Prince may deprive them of their emoluments, without incurring public cenfure—in the
day of his frowns they have no confolation or re-
fource in the favour of the people—if integrity is
wanting, nothing can be expected from fuch men
but unlimited complaifance to the will of the
Prince, and an entire proftitution of their talents
and interefts, to promote whatever fchemes he
may propofe for the advancement of the prerogative. It feems therefore a found, political maxim,
that the Houfes of Parliament cannot go too far
in reftraining the fecret, invifible influence of the
crown. To exclude penfioners altogether from
the Houfe of Commons, excepting thofe who by
long and ufeful fervices have merited of the ftate,
would, I think, be an important additional fecurity to the liberty of the fubject. On the other
hand, I fhould apprehend material injury, if the
number or emoluments of office were fo far re-
trenched, as to afford but fmall profpect of gain to
thofe who devoted their labour and time to the
fervice of the nation in parliament; * becaufe in
fuch a fituation of things there is no reafonable
ground to expect, that the Houfe of Commons
would be improved either with refpect to the morals or abilities of thofe who filled it. A very few

perfons,

---

* A bill for excluding placemen from the Houfe of Commons
was brought in, December 1689, and rejected, and this reafon
affigned, becaufe otherwife the fitteft perfons for ferving their
King and Country would be excluded. It was again brought
in, carried in the Houfe of Commons, but thrown out by the
Peers, January 3, 1692.

perfons, purely difinterefted, might be difpofed to ferve their courtry for its own fake—the far greater number would be prompted to folicit feats in parliament merely by vanity, the ambition of raifing their own confequence, and difplaying their talents at the head of a party. Upon a fair comparifon of the characters of men, and an appeal to experience, I am confident it will be found, that attachment to intereft is a paffion more confiftent with the public welfare, than ambition or the vehement defire of power and diftinction. Intereft may be gratified in the orderly ftate of government, and by the faithful, diligent difcharge of duty—ambition courts popularity, and wifhes for tumult, and has ever occafioned the moft violent outrages upon eftablifhed government. If we compare the more common effects of thofe contrafted characters, it will not admit of any difpute, whether men of frugal habits, who manage their own private affairs with difcretion, and who are mending their fortunes, are not more likely to enter with attention into the affairs of the ftate, to be interefted about the public profperity, and to poffefs, in a higher degree, integrity and fkill, and all the qualifications requifite to form a ftatefman, than thofe men who are carelefs about their own intereft, but poffefs more oftentatious parts, and fucceed better in inveigling the fupport and admiration of the multitude—but the former will never interpofe in the management of public affairs to the damage of their own private fortune. Nor for the fame reafon is it to be wifhed, that the falaries of offices of the greateft importance and truft fhould be fo far curtailed, as to require collateral aid of private fortune to maintain the dignity and rank which belong

long to them, because in that case pretensions to
such offices must be entirely confined to men of
rank and opulence, to the exclusion of more able
and virtuous citizens. Having attended to the
single view in which the influence of the crown
appears to have increased, and pointed out the
remedies which seem most proper to check and
restrain its farther increase, I think it essential to
a fair discussion of the subject, just to hint at a
few circumstances in the present state of the nation, which, without any other means employed,
seem sufficient to counterpoise the accession of
royal power derived from the increase of offices.

First, the prodigious increase of national debt
alone, must prove an unsurmountable limitation
to the ambition of a British Sovereign, supposing
that such ambition really existed. Good humour
is the temper most propitious to beneficence.
When men have been recently successful and are
well pleased, they will sometimes part freely with
more than what is found at an after period to be
either prudent or convenient. And on the contrary, bad fortune, penury and oppression, fret
the temper, and render us ill affected to all around
us. Resentment, at such a season, is often levelled against those whose claims are founded in
law and justice. Because those taxes which are
necessary to pay the interest of the national debt,
and answer the other exigences of the public, are
imposed and executed in the name and by the
authority of the crown, it is but too common for
the ignorant and ill natured, who make a great
part of the whole body of the people, to assign
those evils to the ambition of the Prince, and the
avarice and rapaciousness of his ministers, who are
understood to hold the preference in his favour.

Again,

Again, an independent revenue muſt be the baſis of any ſcheme of extending the prerogative, but the extremity of the nation, and the burden of national debt, deeply felt even by the moſt wealthy, are ſufficient to fruſtrate the plan of accompliſhing an independent revenue or ſubſiſtence to the crown, though the ſentiments of the nation ſhould run ever ſo much in its favour.

But on the contrary, a third check to the increaſing power of the crown, ſprings from the predominant prejudices of the people. The tide of popular opinion runs ſtrong againſt the intereſt and power of the crown. In many inſtances, it even would be dangerous for a Prince to exert his prerogative to the utmoſt verge of law and conſtitution.

The private temper of the Prince was pointed out as another ſource of the increaſe of prerogative. It cannot be doubted, but that a Prince of moderate ambition may deviſe methods, and ſeize opportunities, to extend his prerogative, though neither the prejudices of the people, nor incidental circumſtances, are favourable to his wiſhes. But ſo far from having any reaſon to apprehend danger from this quarter, I now obſerve, that in the known principles and conduct of the Prince who fills the throne, we behold additional ſecurity for the rights and liberties of the people, and may even hope for the amendment of that conſtitution which is the pride of Britain.

Our preſent Sovereign embraced the firſt opportunity to declare, that the rights of his people ſhould be equally dear to him with the moſt valuable prerogatives of his crown. Can the moſt jealous friend of liberty produce one inſtance, in which the conduct of the Prince has deviated from
theſe

thefe declarations, or difappointed the happy expectations which they excited in the minds of the
people. We have now indeed advanced beyond
promifes and declarations. We appeal to experience and to facts. During a reign of twenty
years, as long a period of trial as falls to the
greateft number of Princes, has not the uniform
tenor of his Majefty's government, difplayed the
ftricteft regard to law, to juftice, and the interefts
of his fubjects? Has the moft extravagant licentioufnefs that ever raged in a kingdom which enjoyed the blefling of fettled government, been
able to produce a fhadow of evidence, for affert-
ing that any plan has been deliberately laid, or
that the remoteft inclination of the Sovereign ever
tended to augment the power of the crown, or
infringe the eftablifhed privileges of his people?
Is there in the nation a man of reflection, who
ferioufly apprehends from the temper of the Sovereign, any danger to liberty and the conftitution?
But the grateful citizen will not confine his praifes
to thofe negative virtues, which are fufficient to
remove every ground of jealoufy and diftruft from
the minds of the fubjects — he will account
among the bleffings of heaven, the virtues of the
Prince who claims his loyalty and affection—from
thefe he will trace fubftantial improvements of the
conftitution, and additional fecurity for the liberties of the people *—he will with pleafure dwell
upon

---

* During the prefent reign, the judges have been made independent, and appointed to hold their places for life. General warrants have been declared illegal. The freedom of elections more effectually fecured, by a bill for regulating the pro-
ceedings of the Houfe of Commons on controverted elections,
March 7, 1770.

upon that mildnefs and lenity, which mark every meafure of the reign under which he has been protected—he will obferve with what delicacy and referve, the indifputable prerogatives of the crown have been exercifed—he will admire that liberality and firmnefs which equally difdains the fervices, and defpifes the threats of any party which aims at the monopoly of power—he will read, in every public meafure, a mind that truly becomes a patriot King, fteadily bent upon the great objects of peace and juftice, and national profperity. Good men will fix their eyes with delight, upon thofe amiable domeftic virtues which irradiate a crown, and will be encouraged to hope, that good example, rendered more illuftrious by rank

Are not thefe fubftantial acquifitions to liberty and the confti-tution? The firft and the laft are evident checks upon the power of the crown. The firft of thefe improvements of the conftitution, namely, the rendering the judges independent, proceeded from his Majefty's own gracious propofal. Does it reflect no merit upon the Prince, that the influence of the crown was not exerted to prevent any declaration of the law, contrary to reiterated precedents in the affair of general warrants, which in the cafe of treafon may fometimes be expedient, nay, effential to the fafety of government? Is no praife due to the Prince, that he did not exert his influence to prevent any alteration in the ordinary mode of procedure in the Houfe of Commons, with refpect to the trial of controverted elections, which was to give fuch a mighty blow to minifterial power? Every one ac-quainted with the hiftory of Sir Robert Walpole's adminiftra-tion, may recollect what notorious injuftice was committed in the trial of controverted elections. Indeed, fimilar inftances of injuftice may be imputed to every other adminiftration previous to Mr. Grenville's bill. In determining elections, it was not fo much confidered where the right lay, as to what party the candidates belonged. It is true, the minifter did oppofe Mr. Grenville's bill upon the argument of its inexpediency—but was the crown influence exerted to oppofe it? If it had, muft it not have been effectual to have thrown it out? If not then, furely

the

rank and authority, may yet prove effectual to check that enormous degeneracy of manners, which, more than the combination of the most powerful enemies, threatens the downfal of the British empire.

A period approaches, late may it be 'ere it arrives, when the history of the present reign shall be numbered amongst the records of ages that are past. The clamours of faction, the cavils of discontent, the rage of disappointed ambition shall be heard no more. The name of George the Third shall be written in the fair registers of fame, and stand high in the list of virtuous Princes. Posterity shall blush for the ingratitude of their fathers, and lament that misconstruction and malice, which poisoned the minds of the people, and interrupted the repose of him, who ought to have been among the happiest as well as best of Princes.

the influence of the crown is not so mighty as was represented by gentlemen in opposition upon the sixth of April. Or at any rate, without referring these events to the moderation of the Prince, or running up to the sources and motives from which they sprang, considered merely as facts, do they not exhibit improvements of the constitution, and additional securities for the liberty of the subject?

Amongst the important acquisitions of liberty during this reign, I might have recognised the repeal of the penal statute concerning Roman Catholics; but upon this subject, alas! we are reminded of our shame as well as our honour, and that elevation with which the liberal mind contemplates the extension of liberty, and the enlargement of the legislature, are damped by that more than savage opposition, with which the people have resisted a measure recommended by the first dictates of humanity and justice. I am happy to have lived in an age, and under a government so propitious to toleration; but I blush for human nature, and am humbled in the dust, when conscious of so near a connection with those who, in the eighteenth century, were capable of cherishing an idea of persecution, or cruelty, to any of my fellow creatures.

F I N I S.

www.ingramcontent.com/pod-product-compliance
Lightning Source LLC
Chambersburg PA
CBHW022146090426
42742CB00010B/1411